FOUR
DUBLINERS

Wilde,

Yeats,

Joyce, and

Beckett

FOUR
DUBLINERS

by Richard Ellmann

George Braziller   New York

Published in the United States in 1988 by
George Braziller, Inc.

For information, address the publisher:

George Braziller, Inc.
60 Madison Avenue
New York, New York 10010

These essays were originally presented in somewhat different
form as lectures at the Library of Congress under the
auspices of the Library's Gertrude Clarke Whittall Poetry
and Literature Fund and have been published in
the *New York Review of Books*.

Library of Congress Cataloging-in-Publication Data

Elllmann, Richard, 1918-
  Four Dubliners : Wilde, Yeats, Joyce, and Beckett.

  1. English literature—Irish authors—History and
criticism. 2. Yeats, W. B. (William Butler), 1865-1939.
3. Wilde, Oscar, 1854-1900. 4. Joyce, James, 1882-1941.
5. Beckett, Samuel, 1906-   . 6. Authors, Irish—
Ireland—Dublin (Dublin)—Biography. 7. Dublin (Dublin)
—Intellectual life. 8. Ireland in literature.
I. Title.
[PR8892.D8E57 1987]   820'.9'941835   87-13245
ISBN 0-8076-1208-1

Printed in the United States of America
First Printing, July 1988

To my daughter Maud

Contents

Preface

THESE four Dubliners—Wilde, Yeats, Joyce, and Beckett—were chary of acknowledging their connections. But these connections exist. Some belong to history. Yeats, then eighteen, went to listen to Wilde lecture in 1883; Joyce, at twenty, told Yeats when they first met in 1902 that the poet was too old; Beckett, at twenty-two, was introduced to Joyce in 1928 and became as close a friend as Joyce, not given to intimacy, would allow. On inspection their connections thicken. Wilde and Yeats reviewed each other's work with mutual regard, and sometimes exploited the same themes. Joyce memorialized Wilde as a heroic victim, and repeatedly quoted or referred to him in his later writings. Beckett was saturated in all their works, especially those of Joyce, whose *Anna Livia Plurabelle* he and a friend translated into French.

Yet besides these public admissions of literary kinship, there were affecting personal moments. Wilde invited Yeats to Christmas dinner in 1888 as though Yeats had no family in London, and treated him with great kindness. For his part Yeats circulated a testimonial of support for Wilde at the time of the prosecution for indecent behavior. A few years later Yeats rose at dawn to meet Joyce's train at Euston Station at six o'clock, and after giving the young man breakfast, took him around London editorial offices to find him work. Another scene is of Joyce sitting silent but sympathetic beside Beckett's hospital bed after Beckett had been stabbed.

9

And there is Beckett's surprise and pleasure when, on first meeting Yeats, that poet quoted approvingly some lines from Beckett's *Whoroscope*.

For us the quadrumvirate seem bound together in other ways. They touch successively most areas of our consciousness. Wilde proceeds insouciantly to his doom, and on his way jollies us for being so much harsher than he is, so much less graceful, so much less attractive, and mocks the law for being so witless. Yeats struggles by imaginative passion to overcome the prosaic and to revolutionize reality. Joyce, intransigent yet affirmative, turns the unheroic and mockheroic into the heroic, makes commonplace things lyrical, and undoes church and state. Beckett denies with the same passion that the others affirm, but manifests a sense at times similar to theirs of the comic and incongruous. All four seem, after the manner of modern writers, dislodgers and subverters of everything except truth.

These four, it may be granted, make a strange consortium. Yet resemblances of which they were unaware begin to appear. Displaced, witty, complex, savage, they companion each other. Magnificent, plume-flaunting, sumptuous even in their recognition of aridities, these Dubliners have, like Pythagoras in Yeats's poem, golden thighs. They posit and challenge their own assumptions, they circle from art to anti-art, from delight to horror, from acceptance to renunciation. That they should all come from the same city does not explain them, but they share with their island a tense struggle for autonomy, a disdain for occupation by outside authorities, and a good deal of inner division. These qualities are not exclusively Irish, yet Ireland helps to focus them. And through these four of her natives, Dublin—once reluctantly imperial— regains its power to influence the world through another imperium, that of art.

Richard Ellmann

Emory University
June 27, 1985

FOUR
DUBLINERS

Oscar Wilde by N. Sarony, New York, 1882

Oscar Wilde at Oxford

SCAR WILDE–we have only to hear the name to anticipate that what will be quoted as his will turn conventional solemnities to frivolous insights. So it was in his lifetime, and so it is after his death. Wit, grace, unexpectedness: these are his essence, yet what attracts us too is, as Borges declares, that Wilde is almost always right.

In the process by which Oscar Wilde became Oscar Wilde, his parents must be allowed to have given their impetus. The family into which he was born was intellectually distinguished, and it was also bizarre. Sir William Wilde, his father, started the first eye-and-ear hospital in Ireland and as a surgeon developed these specialties beyond anyone before him. He also trained his own eye on Irish archaeological remains, and his ear on folklore; he brilliantly classified and cataloged the antiquities now in the National Museum of Ireland and collected superstitions and folk tales that might otherwise have been lost. Along with his distinctions and honors went something else: as a young man, before his marriage, he had begotten like some Regency rake three illegitimate children. The secret of who their mothers were was well kept. Oscar Wilde knew his father's children, a fact which may account for the many foundlings and mysteries of birth in his writings. There was nothing predictable about the Wildes' family life.

As for his mother, Lady Wilde, she had broken with her family's Unionist politics by writing vehement poetry in support of the Irish nationalist movement. Her name was Jane, but her pen name was Speranza, because of a highflown genealogical fantasy that her family, the Elgees, were related to Dante's family, the Alighieris. In writing to Longfellow, Dante's translator, she signed herself *Francesca Speranza Wilde*. Later on she became less perfervid as a nationalist; she refused to read the proofs when some of her poems were republished, saying, "I cannot tread the ashes of that once glowing past." But she remained immoderate. In her salon in Dublin, and later in London, she cut a figure in increasingly outlandish costumes, festooned with headdresses and heavy jewelry, and was always capable of making extravagant statements. As her son commented later, "Where there is no extravagance there is no love, and where there is no love there is no understanding." This must serve as a general defense of her conscious rhetoric, and his too. When she moved to London and was asked about her poetry, she sighed, "My singing robes are trailed in London clay." When someone asked her to receive a young woman who was "respectable," she replied, "You must never employ that description in this house. Only tradespeople are respectable." Oscar Wilde remembered this when, in *The Importance of Being Earnest,* Lady Bracknell asks, "Is this Miss Prism a female of repellent aspect, remotely connected with education?" Canon Chasuble replies indignantly, "She is the most cultivated of ladies, and the very picture of respectability." "It is obviously the same person," says Lady Bracknell. Oscar Wilde once commented that his mother and he had decided to found a society for the suppression of virtue, and it says something for their kinship of minds that the idea might have originated with either of them. Lady Wilde delighted Sir William Hamilton, the mathematician, when he was showing her through his big house in Dublin, by saying, "I hope it's haunted." In a more serious moment, when Sir William Wilde was accused in court of having sexually misconducted himself with a woman patient, Lady Wilde—asked why she had taken no notice of the woman's charges against her husband—replied majestically, "I really took no interest in the matter."

That the son of such flamboyant parents should himself have

been flamboyant is no surprise. Wilde was kept at home until he was nine, under private tutors, and then was sent to Portora Royal School in Enniskillen, where he remained until he was sixteen. About these seven years he had nothing to say later, except to reduce them by admitting to only "about one year" at Portora. He must have felt like Mrs. Cheveley in *An Ideal Husband,* who says, "I have forgotten my schooldays. I have a vague impression that they were detestable." Detested Portora nevertheless schooled him in Latin and Greek and sent him on, like other Protestant boys, to Trinity College, Dublin. There he distinguished himself in classics under the tutelage of two rival eminences, Professors Mahaffy and Tyrrell. But after two and a half years Wilde suddenly broke with the expected pattern by taking an examination for a Demyship (scholarship) at Magdalen College, Oxford, and winning it. Professor Mahaffy is reputed to have remarked to him, "You're not quite clever enough for us here, Oscar. Better run up to Oxford."

And so, in October 1874, Wilde traveled from Dublin to the most ancient of British universities. He remained at Oxford for the four years of the Greats course, and a little longer, studying classical history and philosophy as well as literature. An amorphous twenty-year-old boy when he arrived, he was a formed young man of twenty-four when he left. "I have never sowed wild oats," he wrote in a notebook, "I have planted a few orchids." The flower metaphor took firm root.

For Irishmen, Oxford is to the mind what Paris is to the body. Wilde was as receptive as anyone to this fabled equation. The university, gathering in a disproportionate number of the best talents, treated them with a mixture of tenderness and rigor and dispatched them into life forever classified as brilliant, clever, or just average, but Oxford average. The students felt at once affection for this mighty mother and awe of her power to define their lives.

Wilde had no reason to regard himself as a Lucien de Rubem-pré come from the provinces to find in Oxford the great world. Dublin was not Skibbereen. He already knew many Englishmen—artists and actors from England were always attending his mother's Saturday afternoons—and his family name was English. Many of his relations lived in England, and so did friends like Henry Bunbury, who would unwittingly lend his name to Algernon's Bunburying shenanigans in *The Importance of Being Earnest*. The antiquity of Oxford could not have overwhelmed a young man who had accompanied his father on the inspection of prehistoric cromlechs and barrows. Yet Oxford still seemed to be, in Dryden's words, Athens, and everywhere else Thebes. "The most beautiful spot in England," Wilde said of it. Henry James, after a visit there the year before Wilde came up, commented on "the peculiar air of Oxford—the air of liberty to care for intellectual things, assured and secured by machinery which is in itself a satisfaction to sense." Wilde put it more lyrically: he said that being at Oxford was for him "the most flower-like time" in his life.

Still, nostalgia is one thing, and the student world of old Etonians and Wykehamists and Harrovians and incipient Tories another. Wilde presents himself in his writings with a high polish which has been the envy of young people since. But at the start he committed his gaucheries. A friend of his at Balliol, Courtenay Bodley, whom he had met the summer before starting Oxford, drew a malicious but probably accurate portrait of Wilde's early days as an undergraduate. The first time that Wilde dined in hall, according to Bodley, he happened to be seated next to a guest from another college—an athlete in his third year and therefore someone not to be taken lightly. Wilde talked well, and feeling that he had ingratiated himself, as soon as the meal was over presented the athlete with his card, bearing his name and college newly printed. By the unsurmisable rules of Oxford, this was something

Street scene outside Magdalen College, Oxford

*A. F. Peyton, C. H. Lindon (in front), C. H. Tindale, Wilde (hatted), and
J. J. Peyton, March 13, 1875*

that was not done. Rebuffed on this occasion, and no doubt on others, Wilde determined to be ahead of rather than behind the English. His Dublin accent disappeared in favor of that stately and distinct English, phrased in perfect sentences, which so astonished Yeats and others later. He developed a great appetite for formal wear, and told a friend, "If I were alone on a desert island and had my things, I should dress for dinner every night." (Who would cook for him he did not consider.) In the daytime, he put aside his Dublin clothing and became sportier than his friends by donning tweed jackets with even larger checks than theirs, bird's-eye-blue neckties, tall collars, curly-brimmed hats balanced on one ear. His thick brown hair was cut acceptably short at Spiers's Barber Shop in the High. This was only the first phase of his sartorial revolution; it would be succeeded a couple of years later by a more sophisticated dandyism, involving a coat cut in the shape of a cello and similar flourishes.

His appearance and his conversation quickly made Wilde conspicuous. He annoyed thereby those who hated conspicuousness but amused and pleased his friends, who recognized in him an element of self-mocking excess. There are many examples of his conviviality with contemporaries and of his insolence to his putative superiors. One report by a proctor, dated November 1, 1875, complained that Wilde and three other men had been found dining at the Clarendon—evidently a heinous offense. The proctor took their names and instructed them to finish their meal as quickly as possible and report to his college, Jesus. They kept asking him, "Shall we report to Jesus?" until he departed, much annoyed. He returned a quarter of an hour later to find them still there. "They were, if possible, still ruder than before," he noted. "Wilde strutted about the room with his hat on"—no doubt one of those curly-brimmed ones of which he was proud—until the proctor instructed him to remove it. The proctor proposed that they should all be gated, that is, confined to their colleges.

Wilde seems to have enjoyed subverting authority. At the Divinity examination which he had to take at the end of his second year, he went up to the proctor to obtain the examination paper. The proctor inquired, "Are you taking Divinity or Substituted Matter?" (The substituted matter was for non-Anglicans.) "Oh, the Forty-Nine Articles," Wilde replied indifferently. "The Thirty-Nine, you mean, Mr. Wilde," said the proctor. "Oh, is it really?" asked Wilde in his weariest manner. (He would talk later of the Twenty Commandments; by miscounting them he discounted them.) The examiner on this occasion was W. H. Spooner, later Warden of New College. Spooner reproved Wilde for being late, to which Wilde replied airily, "You must excuse me. I have no experience of these pass examinations," meaning that an examination in which one simply passed or failed was beneath his notice. Spooner, himself in orders and a nephew of the Archbishop of Canterbury, reprimanded him by telling him to copy out the 26th chapter of Acts in Greek. After a time, seeing that Wilde was toiling away industriously, Spooner relented. "You have done enough." But Wilde continued to write. Spooner said, "Did you hear me tell you, Mr. Wilde, that you needn't write any more?" "Oh yes, I heard," said Wilde, "but I was so interested in what I was copying that I could not leave off. It was all about a man named Paul, who went on a voyage and was caught in a terrible storm, and I was afraid that he would be drowned; but do you know, Mr. Spooner, he was saved; and when I found that he was saved, I thought of coming to tell you." Another version of this incident says that Spooner asked Wilde to construe from Greek those verses in Matthew which record the betrayal of the Saviour by Judas for thirty pieces of silver. After Wilde had construed a few verses, Spooner stopped him. "Very good, that will do, Mr. Wilde." "Hush, hush," replied the candidate, raising an admonitory finger, "let us proceed and see what happened to the unfortunate man." It is hard to choose between legends, but clear that Wilde was already creating his own. It was also clear that the examiner was not amused. "I was ploughed, of course," Wilde informed a friend. He had to take the examination over again.

On another occasion, it was his turn to read the lesson at Magdalen College chapel on a day when Queen Victoria's youngest son, Leopold, was present. Wilde leafed over the pages and began in a languorous voice, "The Song of Solomon." The dean of the college swooped down from his stall and thrusting his beard into Wilde's face said, "You have the wrong lesson, Mr. Wilde. It is Deuteronomy 16." In later life Wilde remembered that he had

*Wilde with Magdalen College friends Reginald Harding and William
Ward, March 12, 1876*

Walter Pater. Engraving based on a drawing by Simeon Solomon, 1872

always read the lesson with an air of skepticism and was invariably reproved for "levity at the lectern."

He was similarly intransigent when he was haled before the Vice-Chancellor's Court in November 1877 for nonpayment of two debts to shopkeepers. Wilde was fined a pound for one debt, but three pounds for the other, which was larger. He thereupon wrote a letter to the vice-chancellor protesting that the larger fine was "extortionate and exorbitant," and suggesting that "the Vice Chancellor's court must be conducted on a system which requires the investigation of the University Commission." In all the long history of the Vice-Chancellor's Court, probably no other undergraduate had ever alleged that it was corrupt.

Wilde did not, however, allow himself to do badly in his first public examinations, which came in 1876, or the end of his second year. Secretly he must have studied a little, for he got a first. He was pleased to demonstrate his academic brilliance but aspired to larger distinction. For this he knew he must sort out the intellectual universe with which Oxford confronted him. To Wilde the two principal people at Oxford, and the ones he said he most wanted to meet, were John Ruskin and Walter Pater. For an undergraduate with artistic tastes, they were the inevitable centers of attention. Ruskin, at fifty-five, occupied the respected position of Slade Professor of Fine Art; Pater, thirty-five, a fellow of Brasenose College, tried but failed to become his successor. Wilde cannot have known in advance how opposed to each other they were: Pater, once Ruskin's disciple, disagreed with his master without naming him; Ruskin loftily ignored Pater's aspirations to rival him.

Wilde did not meet Pater in person until his third year at Oxford, but during his first term he came under the spell of his *Studies in the History of the Renaissance,* published a few months before. He never ceased to speak of it as "my golden book," and in *De Profundis* said it was "the book which has had such a strange influence over my life." Much of it, especially the celebrated conclusion, he had by heart. Pater declared that, life being a drift of momentary acts, we must cultivate each moment to the full, seeking "not the fruit of experience, but experience itself" as our goal. In *The Picture of Dorian Gray* Dorian embraces this doctrine as his own in exactly these words without acknowledgment, as if to his other crimes he was adding that of plagiarism. Success in life is to "burn always with this hard gemlike flame," said Pater—Wilde now adopted *flamelike* as one of his favorite adjectives. We can burn variously, through the passions (of which Pater strongly approved), through political or religious enthusiasms or what he called the religion of humanity, and best of all, through art. To expose all the sensibilities as fully as possible was an ideal that attracted Wilde, though he indicated reservations when he had Lord Henry Wotton talk this kind of Paterese to Dorian Gray with evident ill effects.

Ruskin had made England art-conscious through a different approach, in which morality played a major part. Artists could display their morality by fidelity to nature and by eschewing self-indulgent sensuality. The word *aesthetic* became a bone of contention between Ruskin's disciples and Pater's. Though Ruskin sometimes used the term favorably, to apply to various aspects of artistic discrimination, he was enraged when it was used to justify amoral art. As early as 1846 he denounced the aesthetic as a slogan that degraded the arts into mere amusements, "ticklers and fanners of the soul's sleep." But in 1868 Pater commended the Pre-Raphaelites for being the "Aesthetic School of Poetry." Responding to Pater and his followers in 1883, Ruskin declared that the growing habit of calling aesthetic what was only "pigs-flavouring of pigs' wash" argued a "moral deficiency." His art criticism always harked back to the medieval period, with its faith and its Gothic, while he argued that the Renaissance, the more it bloomed, the more it decayed. Wilde accepted this point of view in *De Profundis*. But what he read in Pater was different: for Pater the medieval period was valued only as an anticipation of the Renaissance, and the best of the Renaissance was still going on. As for decadence, Pater did not shrink from welcoming what he called "a refined and comely decadence."

Wilde could see that he was being offered not only two very different doctrines but two very different vocabularies. Though both Ruskin and Pater favored beauty, for Ruskin it had to be allied with good. For Pater it might have ever so slight a touch of evil—he rather liked the Borgias, for example. Ruskin spoke of faith; Pater spoke of mysticism, as if for him religion became bearable only when it overflowed into excess. Ruskin appealed to conscience, Pater to imagination. Ruskin invoked disciplined restraint, Pater allowed for a pleasant drift. What Ruskin loathed as vice, Pater caressed as wantonness.

Wilde was as concerned for his soul as for his body, and however titillated he was by Pater, he looked to Ruskin for spiritual guidance. He made a point of attending Ruskin's lectures in 1874 on Florentine art. Ruskin was apt to interrupt his description of a painting by exhorting his hearers to do something, such as to fall in love at the first opportunity. He reminded them that the previous spring he had proposed that instead of developing their bodies in pointless games, in "fruitless slashing of the river," in learning "to leap and to row, to hit a ball with a bat," they should join him in improving the countryside. Where there had been nothing but a malarial swamp at North Hinksey, they should help him to construct a flower-bordered country road. It was to be an ethical adventure like building a gothic cathedral, rather than narcissistic athleticism.

Although Wilde found rising at dawn more difficult than most men—his mother never rose till afternoon—he overcame his languor for Ruskin's sake. Later he bragged comically that he had enjoyed the distinction of being allowed to fill "Mr. Ruskin's especial wheelbarrow," and of being instructed by the master himself in the mysteries of wheeling such an object from place to place. The road was then in process of being paved, digging having been accomplished the previous spring. It was not much of a road, but it was for Wilde the road to Ruskin, who invited his sweaty workers to breakfast after their exertions. The work went on to the end of term, after which Ruskin was off to Venice, and Wilde could again lie late abed, as the road for its part slowly sank from sight. No trace of it remains.

His friendship with Ruskin was gratifying and instructive. He would write to him later, "The dearest memories of my Oxford days are my walks and talks with you, and from you I learned nothing but what was good." During his early days at Oxford he seems consciously to have imitated Ruskin's views. Ruskin had said, "At Paddington station I felt as if in hell." Wilde as his disciple told friends that all the factory chimneys and vulgar workshops should be taken up and placed on some out-of-the-way island. "I would give Manchester back to the shepherds and Leeds to the stockfarmers," he magnanimously announced. Thanks to Ruskin, Wilde did not fall into the individualistic aestheticism favored by Pater; from the start he argued as Ruskin did that art had a role in the improvement of society.

For Wilde, by the time he reached Oxford, aestheticism was a familiar subject, bordering on staleness. At Trinity College he had already been caricatured as an indignant aesthete, and his brother Willie had read a paper to an undergraduate society—of which Oscar was also a member—on the subject of "Aesthetic Morality." Lady Wilde had translated from the German an interminable novel which portrayed the presumption and failure of a kind of aesthete. In fact, the use of the term aestheticism was as controversial in the 1870s as is that of post-structuralism today. Wilde speaks in a letter of 1875 with some irony of a classmate as an "aesthetic" young man, and his literary tastes were at times for something quite unaesthetic and earnest, such as Mrs. Browning's *Aurora Leigh,* which like Ruskin he praised inordinately. During his second year at Oxford, Wilde read with great amusement the attack on aestheticism—and particularly on Pater's form of it—in W. H. Mallock's *The New Republic.* He could see that aestheticism was going out as much as it was coming in; though he adopted many of its interests, such as tints and textures, he did so always with something of his mother's high-spiritedness, which, while excessive, poked fun at its own excess. It was in this tone that he made his famous remark, "I find it harder and harder to live up to my blue china." Four years later *Punch* would fix on this as part of its campaign against aestheticism, but Wilde had obviously said it with some self-mockery. Still, to live up to one's blue china is not so absurd as it may sound—we have all much to learn from our bricabrac.

John Ruskin. Engraving by J. A. O'Neill

The letters he wrote at Oxford say less about aestheticism than they do about Catholicism. Wilde knew that Ruskin had spent the summer before they met in a monastic cell at Assisi. Pater used to visit Roman Catholic churches to admire the ceremonies and decorations, and in *Marius the Epicurean* he would praise their "aesthetic charm." Still, Wilde was more tempted by the Church than either Pater or Ruskin, and for two and a half years thought of making one among the distinguished Oxford converts, who included Manning, Newman, and, more recently, Gerard Manley Hopkins. At Magdalen he met a young man who brought the issue home to him.

This was David Hunter Blair, from a titled Scottish family, later to become a Benedictine abbot. During the winter term of 1875 he obtained leave to study music in Leipzig, and from Leipzig proceeded to Rome in time to attend the ceremony at which Manning was created a cardinal, on March 15, 1875. Ten days later Hunter Blair was himself received into the Church. Pius IX treated his conversion as a notable one, and conferred on him the honorary post of papal chamberlain. No sooner was Hunter Blair back at Oxford than he began to urge Wilde and others to follow him into the Church. Several Magdalen students did. Wilde protested that his father would cut him off if he took any such step, but he acceded sufficiently to fill his room, by June 1875, with photographs of the pope and Cardinal Manning.

During the summer that followed Wilde made his first trip to Italy, in the company of his old professor J. P. Mahaffy. He began to write poems, and their theme was his equal temptation to pursue the spiritual and the profane. In one, "San Miniato," he celebrates Fra Angelico, but it is Fra Angelico among the nightingales—the attraction of secularism being explicit; at the end he prays to the Virgin Mary to show him mercy before "the scorching sun / Show to the world my sin and shame." When the poem was published, his mother, as a professional poet, made the objection,

"Sin is respectable and highly poetical but shame is not." But Wilde had borrowed the phrase from an even more professional poet, Tennyson (*In Memoriam,* 48).

On his return to Oxford in the autumn of 1875, Wilde continued to dally with conversion. On November 23, Cardinal Manning came to dedicate the new church of St. Aloysius in St. Giles', the first Catholic church to be built in Oxford since the Reformation. Wilde's name appears among those who listened to the cardinal denounce the spiritual apathy and decay of Oxford, and he spoke of Manning as "my favorite preacher." In December he went to see his friend Bodley in Balliol and said that he was "swaying between Romanism…and Atheism." Bodley acidly reminded him that one Irish papist the more would not disturb the world. Wilde continued to sway. "I think since Christ the dead world has woke up from sleep," he wrote to a friend. The summer following he carried certain of Newman's books with him to Ireland, though he visited on Newman some of his own doubts and later described him as "that troubled soul in its progress from darkness to darkness."

Swaying between Catholicism and atheism, Wilde adopted for a time another creed or near creed—Freemasonry. In his first year at Oxford, Bodley had persuaded Wilde to join the Apollo Lodge of the Freemasons. It was a fashionable thing to do, because Queen Victoria's son Leopold, at Christ Church, was head of the order. At first Wilde took the craft lightly as a social club, but gradually he became more involved. When he had finished the preliminary degrees he had to decide whether to proceed, like his friend Bodley, into the Apollo Royal Arch Chapter or to follow a somewhat more unusual path into the Apollo Rose Croix Chapter. The difference was that the Rose Croix was High Church, with a ritual that dealt explicitly with Christ's death and resurrection and included a communion rite. Wilde chose to take the latter course on November 27, 1876, that is, in his third Oxford year. "I have got rather keen on Freemasonry lately," he wrote on March 3, 1877, "and believe in it awfully." The adverb suggests some self-mockery. He goes on, "in fact [I] would be awfully sorry to have to give it up in case I secede from the Protestant Heresy." With missionary zeal he sponsored four Magdalen students into the order. But in the same letter he indicates how various his inclinations were:

I now breakfast with Father Parkinson, go to St Aloysius, talk sentimental religion to Dunlop [one of Hunter Blair's converts] and altogether am caught in the fowler's snare, in the wiles of the Scarlet Woman—I may go over in the vac. I have dreams of a visit to Newman, of the holy sacrament in a new church, and of a quiet and peace afterwards in my soul. I need not say, though, that I shift with every breath of thought and am weaker and more self-deceiving than ever.

If I could hope that the Church would wake in me some earnestness and purity I would go over *as a luxury,* if for no better reason. But I can hardly hope it would, and to go over to Rome would be to sacrifice and give up my two great gods "Money and Ambition."

Still I get so wretched and troubled that in some desperate mood I will seek the shelter of a church which simply enthrals me by its fascination.

It was just after writing this letter that he was prevailed upon by Hunter Blair to visit Rome. Wilde had no money, but Hunter Blair—a wealthy man—promised on the way to meet his parents to stop at Monte Carlo and put two pounds on a number in Wilde's name. Soon sixty pounds arrived, ostensibly Hunter Blair's winnings. It seemed that Wilde had no choice but to go. "This is an era in my life, a crisis," he wrote to a friend. He qualified his acceptance, however, by arranging with Professor Mahaffy, who was taking two young men with him to Greece, to accompany them as far as Genoa. On the way there, Mahaffy as an arch-Protestant attempted to alter Wilde's resolution to visit Rome by inviting him to Greece. Wilde was firm. Then Mahaffy said sternly, "I won't take you. I wouldn't have such a fellow with me." Proof against argument, Wilde was not proof against disdain. He agreed to go to Greece, but with the proviso that he would leave the Mahaffy party in Athens and return by way of Rome. It was a characteristic decision: as between alternatives he chose both.

Pagan Greece had something of the subversive effect upon Papal Rome that Mahaffy desired. Wilde, by the time he finally

Wilde in Greek costume, Greece, March 1877

joined Hunter Blair in Rome, was veering away from Catholicism. But Hunter Blair arranged for him a momentous meeting with Pope Piux IX. The pope urged him to follow his condiscipulus (so popes talk) into the city of God. Wilde found the meeting awesome; he said not a word, closeted himself in his hotel room, and emerged with a sonnet which gave Hunter Blair heart. But poems are not so good as prayers. That same afternoon, as they were driving by the Protestant cemetery, Wilde insisted upon stopping their carriage and then, to Hunter Blair's dismay, prostrated himself before the grave of Keats. It was a humbler obeisance than he had given to the pope. After this Hunter Blair refused to read any more sonnets.

Another force in Wilde's mind was working against Catholicism as effectively as paganism or aestheticism. This was the profane life of the senses in a much less generalized mode. Wilde's sexuality teetered between love of women and love of men. During his second year at Oxford he became engaged to a young woman in Dublin named Florence Balcombe, but after two years she broke off their understanding and was married to Bram Stoker, later the author of *Dracula*. Various other young women fell in and out of Wilde's life during this time—he was obviously flirtatious, and with women. Still, his male friendships included some that were equivocal. On December 4, 1875, his friend Bodley noted in a diary, "Called on Wilde, who leaves foolish letters from people who are 'Hungry' for him and call him 'Fosco' for his friends to read." Evidently Wilde saw no reason to be secretive.

Not long afterwards, however, there occurred an incident which had many repercussions. An undergraduate at Balliol named William Money Hardinge, whom Wilde knew as one of Ruskin's roadbuilders, was disclosed to have received letters from Walter Pater signed, "Yours lovingly." Hardinge had also written and circulated some homosexual poems. The affair was brought to the attention of the authorities by Balliol students who feared that the "Balliol Bugger," as Hardinge was called, was giving the college a bad name. Early in 1876 the master of Balliol, Benjamin Jowett, was apprised of the Pater letters and the sonnets. He now broke with Pater—a famous rupture—and had Hardinge up on the official charge of "keeping and reciting immoral poetry." Hardinge denied it at first, but when threatened with a proctorial inquiry agreed to resign from the college. Eleven years later Wilde would review one of Hardinge's novels and comment good-humoredly that its hero was "an Arcadian Antinous and a very Ganymede in gaiters."

Though Wilde was not himself involved with Hardinge, he had begun to evince the same interest in inversion that he was showing in conversion. André Raffalovich, an unfriendly witness, says that Wilde boasted of taking as much pleasure in talking about the subject of homosexuality as others had in practicing it. The summer after Hardinge had to decamp, in 1876, Wilde noticed another Oxford student named Todd sitting with a choir boy in a private box at Dublin theater. He confided the matter to a friend in Magdalen, but added, "Don't tell anyone about it like a good boy—it would do neither us nor Todd any good." In this case he showed caution, but he was incautious enough to form a friendship with Lord Ronald Gower, a sculptor who was patently homosexual but so well connected that nobody noticed. And this same year, Wilde wrote a letter to Oscar Browning, who had been dismissed as a master at Eton because of alleged over-intimacy with a prize pupil, and asked to meet him because, he said, "I have heard you so much abused that I am sure you must be a most excellent person."

Wilde was taking risks. The following year, 1877, he published his first prose, a review of the opening of the new Grosvenor Gallery in London. The review put great emphasis upon paintings of boys and included the telltale sentences: "In the Greek islands boys can be found as beautiful as the Charmides of Plato. Guido's 'St Sebastien' in the Palazzo Rossi at Genoa is one of these boys, and Perugino once drew a Greek Ganymede for his native town, but the painter who most shows the influence of this type is Correggio, whose lily-bearer in the cathedral at Parma, and whose wild-eyed, open-mouthed St John in the 'incoronata Madonna' of St Giovanni Evangelista, are the best examples in art of the bloom and vitality and radiance of this adolescent beauty." Sure that Pater would like this article, Wilde sent it to him, and was at once invited to their first meeting. The same year there appeared an anonymous pamphlet entitled *Boy Worship at Oxford,* reflecting the propensity that Wilde and Pater shared.

Yet just as he was dallying with Freemasonry at the same time as with Catholicism, which was opposed to it, so Wilde appears to have kept to heterosexual practices while clearly tending in another direction. It was at Oxford, probably, that an event took place which was to alter his life. Arthur Ransome wrote in his life of Wilde in 1911, on the basis of information from Robert Ross, that Wilde had syphilis, and that the ear infection from which he died in 1900 was related to paresis. Reggie Turner, also with Wilde in his last days, wrote the same thing, and added that the doctor in charge had ultimately so diagnosed Wilde's malady. It was said in the Wilde circle that he had contracted the disease while at Oxford from a woman prostitute. A mysterious illness in March of his fourth year may have been the onset of the disease, which on medical advice he is said to have treated—as was then customary— with mercury. In "The Sphinx," a poem which Ross said Wilde had begun at Oxford, there occur the lines: "Are there not others more accursed, whiter with leprosies than I?" The allusion is to the leprosy about which Naaman, the Syrian captain in the Old Testament, consults the prophet Elisha. (Wilde's interest in this figure continued: he gave his name to the executioner in *Salome.*) It may well have been the onset of syphilis which led him the next month, that is, in April 1878, to consult the society priest of the day, the Reverend Sebastian Bowden, at the Brompton Oratory in London. The possibility of being purged of his sin seems to have emerged at the interview, because in a letter of Father Bowden which has survived, the priest says, "Let me repeat to you as solemnly as I can what I said yesterday, you have like everyone else an evil nature and this in your case has become more corrupt by bad influences mental and moral, and by positive sin; hence you speak as a dreamer and sceptic with no faith in anything and no purpose in life." Positive sin sounds like a heterosexual offense rather than something perverse. Father Bowden ended his letter by inviting Wilde to return to the Brompton Oratory to be received into the Church: "I trust that you will come on Thursday and have another talk; you may be quite sure I shall urge you to do nothing but what your conscious dictates. In the meantime pray hard and talk little." He knew his man.

At last Wilde had been brought to the point of decision. Although Bowden's letter has been available for some time, what Wilde did in response to it has not been known. But Father Bowden told André Raffalovich, himself a convert, what happened next. On the Thursday, when Wilde was to be received into the Church, there arrived at the Brompton Oratory, instead of Wilde, a large package. On being opened this proved to contain a bunch of lilies. It was Wilde's polite way of flowering over his renunciation. What he would say of Dorian Gray was true of himself: "It was rumoured of him [Dorian] that he was about to join the Roman Catholic communion; and certainly the Roman ritual had a great attraction for him...But he never fell into the error of arresting his intellectual development by any formal acceptance of creed or system, or of mistaking, for a house in which to live, an inn that is but suitable for the sojourn of a night in which there are no stars and the moon is in travail...no theory of life seemed to him to be of any importance compared with life itself." Wilde evidently decided that he must accept mercury rather than religion as the specific for his dreadful disease.

And now we begin to recognize how Wilde brought himself to full consciousness at Oxford. He had begun by stirring his conscience with Ruskin and his senses with Pater; these worthies had gradually passed into more complicated blends of Catholicism, Freemasonry, aestheticism, and various kinds of behavior, all embraced fervently but impermanently. At first, as his letters reveal, he tried to resolve his own contradictions and berated himself for being weak and self-deceiving. But gradually while at Oxford he came to see his contradictions as sources of strength rather than volatility. In a world where "the dullard and the

doctrinaire" limited themselves, as he said, by grand decisions
about their beliefs, he declined to do so. "A truth in art is that
whose contradictory is also true," he would declare in "The Truth
of Masks." This was the great lesson which his immersion in
various movements had taught him, first about art, then about life.
He would be neither a Catholic nor a Freemason; aesthetic one
moment, he would be anaesthetic the next. This conclusion jibed
with what was perhaps involuntary, his oscillation between the
love of women and of men.

As a result, Wilde's works are written out of a debate between
doctrines rather than out of doctrine. In "Hélas!," the poem with
which he prefaced his first book of verse, he indicates that in
yielding to pleasure he has not given up his austerity, that the
heights as well as the depths still attract him. In his first play, *Vera,*
the heroine plans to kill the Czar, but instead saves his life, as if she
had suddenly been made aware of her own contradictory impulse
and decided not to resist it. When Wilde writes a sonnet about
political revolutionaries, he disparages them in the octave but at
the end of the sestet is suddenly minded to say, "God knows it I am
with them, in some things." *The Picture of Dorian Gray* is a critique
of aestheticism, which is shown to bring Dorian to ruin; yet
readers have been won by Dorian's beauty and regretful, rather
than horrified, at his waste of it, so that he has something of the
glamor of a Faust rather than the foulness of a murderer and drug
addict. And Wilde, feeling that the book had too much moral,
added to it a preface which expounds sympathetically some of that
aesthetic creed by which the book shows Dorian to be corrupted.
In *Salome* Wilde allows King Herod to yield first to sensual delec-
tation as he watches Salome dance the dance of the seven veils,
then to horrified jealousy as he watches her kiss the dead lips of
Iokanaan, and finally to outraged conscience as he orders the
guards to kill her. Lady Windermere has to discover that for all her
puritanism she is capable like other people of doing something
utterly averse to her principles. In *An Ideal Husband* Lady Chiltern
has to reconcile herself to the fact that ideal husbands may have
concealed real secrets. In *The Importance of Being Earnest* Wilde
might be said to parody his own tendency to look for contradictions by having serious Jack turn out to be frivolous Ernest. "The

wise contradict themselves," Wilde declares in his "Phrases and Philosophies for the Use of the Young," and in *De Profundis,* which he wrote in prison, he offers himself as a penitent but in this guise begins to turn into a martyr, to be released and reborn and justified. In his last work, *The Ballad of Reading Gaol,* the hero of which has slit his wife's throat with a razor, Wilde suddenly turns upon his hypocrite readers to say that we are all murderers of the thing we love.

This sudden perception of a truth opposed to the home truth we are all prepared to acknowledge, and just as plausible, was Wilde's answer to what he called the "violence of opinion" exhibited as he saw by most of his contemporaries. He traced his own detachment from that violence to Oxford, where he said he had learned "the Oxford temper," though it was really his own temper. By the time he left the university he could see that life's complexity could not easily be codified into thirty-nine or forty-nine articles, into ten or twenty commandments, into pluses and minuses awarded to this person or that creed. Wilde was a moralist, in a school where Blake, Nietzsche, and even Freud were his fellows. The object of life is not to simplify it. As our conflicting impulses coincide, as our repressed feelings vie with those we express, as our solid views disclose unexpected fissures, we are all secret dramatists, whether or not we bring our complexities onto the stage. In this light Wilde's works become exercises in self-criticism as well as pleas for tolerance.

William Bulter Yeats, 1932

W. B. Yeats's Second Puberty

W. B. YEATS, and not I, described his last years as a second puberty. He meant the term to express his renewed sexual vigor, though he thought of it as also a psychological recovery. Just after his marriage, when he was fifty-two, he had written in a poem, "I have as healthy flesh and blood as any rhymer's had," yet things had changed by the time he reached sixty-eight. At that time, in 1934, he complained to a friend that his sexual powers had diminished. The friend, as much in jest as in earnest, remarked that an Austrian physiologist, Eugen Steinach, had developed in 1918 an operation for rejuvenation. It had become popular in the 1920s. In Vienna, for example, a hundred teachers and university professors had submitted to the operation, one of them being Freud (though not for sexual reasons) in 1923. Yeats promptly went to the library to consult the one book in English that dealt with it, *Rejuvenation* (1924), by the London surgeon Norman Haire. Haire wrote that he himself at that time had performed twenty-five such operations, with what he regarded as generally good results. The operation lasted only a quarter of an hour. No monkey glands took part. It was what we now know as a vasectomy: the surgeon cut the vas deferens, removed a piece of it, then tied up the two ends separately. Steinach's theory, which unfortunately is no longer held, was that the production of the male hormone would thereby be increased and vitalize the whole body's functioning.

39

Norman Haire was a well-known figure in London sexological circles. Yeats went to consult him and told him—as Haire wrote to me twelve years later—"that for about three years...he had lost all inspiration and been unable to write anything new. He had gone over varying versions of his poems, choosing those he preferred." To rescue his verse as well as his potency, then, Yeats thought he must undergo the operation. (He spoke also of improving his blood pressure.) Versemaking and lovemaking were always connected in his mind. Not to be able to do the one meant not to be able to do the other. In a late poem he declares that the spur of his poetry has always been lust and rage, the same qualities which in "Byzantium" he speaks of as "the fury and the mire of human veins." What awakened his images to life, he insisted in a song for *The King of the Great Clock Tower,* was "heroic wantonness."

Haire operated on his distinguished patient during the first week of April 1934. Was the operation a success? Yeats thought that it was and must have encouraged his friend, the poet Sturge Moore, to have it two years later. On the physical level it cannot have had much effect, for Norman Haire, whom Yeats authorized to discuss his case, said to me what a woman friend of Yeats's confirmed—my curiosity was I hope legitimized by my being one of Yeats's biographers—that the operation had no effect upon his sexual competence. He could not have erections, Haire told me. But the effect on his mind, as Mrs. Yeats emphasized to me eight years after his death, was incalculable. Subsequent to the operation Yeats wrote to Norman Haire (as Haire remembered) that "he had written new poems which, in the opinion of those whose opinion he valued most, were among his best work." These were poems included in the volume called *A Full Moon in March.*

The operation alarmed Yeats's friends. Frank O'Connor imagined that it was like putting a Cadillac engine in a Ford car. Yeats supposed that it had put an additional strain on his constitution. In a letter to Dorothy Wellesley of June 17, 1935, a letter she omitted from their published correspondence, he wrote, "I find my present weakness made worse by the strange second puberty the operation has given me, the ferment that has come upon my imagination. If I write more poetry it will be unlike anything I have done." He was projecting the volume we know as *Last Poems,* in which he would speak as "a wild old wicked man," "a foolish passionate man," and express what he called "an old man's frenzy," a frenzy that privileged him to speak out.

Yeats had only five years to live. He craved sexual intimacy and found several women willing to share it, whatever its limitations, yet he was always the writer, doing things as much "for the song's sake" as for other reasons. His wife said to him (and repeated her comment to Edith Shackleton Heald), "When you are dead people will talk about your love affairs, but I shall say nothing, for I will remember how proud you were." He was determined to make his last years count. What I shall contend here is that they constitute, notwithstanding all the reverberations of a long lifetime, a distinct period, a phase in which Yeats treats old subjects with greater explicitness and freedom and greater awareness of ultimate implications. He seems determined to cultivate extravagance, as if at their utmost bound things took on at last their true shapes and colors.

In *Last Poems* Yeats presents a spectrum of polymorphous sexual possibility. For example, there are two pairs of ideal lovers, Peleus and Thetis and the Irish Baile and Ailinn, whose resurrected bodies recreate their old earthy passions. On this side of mortality, too, the same impulses seek or achieve satisfaction. Yeats's spokesman is often an old man who ranges from longing to be young again and to hold a girl in his arms to swishing around with a pretty punk, chatting with an old bawd, and claiming to be "a young man in the dark." When Yeats turns again to his old beloved Maud Gonne, always the central figure in his poetical enterprise, he does something with her that he has never done before—he names her. For the first time, as she waits for a train at Howth station, she is taken out of legend for a moment and put into life. The same candor appears in his vocabulary. Cuchulain's wife is now given the Homeric epithet of "great-bladdered Emer." Long before Yeats had been bold enough to speak of "the worse devil that is between my thighs," but now, in the sequence of "The Three Bushes," he talks even more explicitly of "the lover's rod and its butting head," and describes it after intercourse as "weak as a worm." In the Crazy Jane poems he had spoken grandly and

Latinately of "the place of excrement"; in the *Last Poems* this becomes just "bum":

> Foul goat-head, brutal arm appear,
> Belly, shoulder, bum,
> Flash fishlike; nymphs and satyrs
> Copulate in the foam

Such diversions go on in heaven itself, Yeats reports in "News for the Delphic Oracle," as if heaven too had had a Steinach operation performed by the poet himself.

He salts other subjects in the same way. Long ago he had celebrated the Easter Rebellion of 1916, memorialized its martyrs, and proclaimed that because of it "A terrible beauty is born." Now, in the 1930s, he finds nothing to praise in the regime of the Easter rebel, De Valera, whom like Maud Gonne he names. His attitude towards fascism is similar. He imagined briefly in 1933 that Ireland might have found a worthier leader in General O'Duffy, leader of the Blue Shirts, but soon turned against him and wrote, "What if there's nothing up there at the top?" For good measure, in a poem addressed to those clerics and fascists who supposed that strengthening Church and State would put down the mob, he wrote,

> What if the Church and the State
> Are the mob that howls at the door!

Not content with this, Yeats wrote still another poem, "The Great Day," dissociating himself from all governments:

> Hurrah for revolution and more cannon-shot!
> A beggar upon horseback lashes a beggar on foot.
> Hurrah for revolution and cannon come again!
> The beggars have changed places, but the lash goes on.

The elegiac tone with which in the twenties he had lamented the loss of the old order changes to a kind of lambasting of "the sort now growing up, / All out of shape from toe to top," including aristocracy, middle class, and peasants alike.

42

The five years left to Yeats following the Steinach operation were a period of great literary fecundity. He wrote a series of works in prose and verse. There were four verse plays, more outspoken than their predecessors. The first, *A Full Moon in March,* centered on the beheading of a poet. Then *The Herne's Egg* dealt with the rape of a priestess by seven men. In *Purgatory* an old man, who long ago killed his father, now kills his own son. In *The Death of Cuchulain,* the figure whose heroic deeds Yeats had celebrated in other plays dies at last with more indignity than glory at a fool's hand. Yeats now composed the last section of his *Autobiographies* and varied his usual loftiness of tone by a gossipy exposure of the foibles of George Moore. He also compiled *The Oxford Book of Modern Verse,* in which he praised and dispraised various contemporaries to excess and—in this most tendentious of all the Oxford Books—included great swatches of obscure poets to whom he alone was partial. He prepared, too, a collected edition of his writings and, in an introduction to it, surprised his potential readers by such remarks as, "I am no nationalist, except in Ireland for passing reasons"—this from a lifelong nationalist who in his last poems would speak of "We Irish" and address himself to "Irish poets" as if he were very much one of them. In what he intended to be the first installment of a series called *On the Boiler*—the title drawn from a recollection of a ship's carpenter who harangued from on top of a boiler in Sligo—Yeats polemicized against modern education, plumped for eugenics, and in general claimed to be discarding his usual "patter" in favor of the fanaticism which it had always overlain. No statement was too willful: he announced that a small Irish army "could throw back from our shores the disciplined uneducated masses of the commercial nations." Mrs. Yeats told me that in the second number of *On the Boiler,* which he did not live to write, he intended to fulminate against all institutional religions.

This sounds like "a wild old man" indeed, and yet Yeats is so inevitably a writer that neither his art nor his audience seems ever in danger of being forgotten. One of his principal undertakings in

43

his last years was to prepare a new edition of his book *A Vision,* the most eccentric of all his writings. The first edition, published in 1926, contained two sections that were in finished form, but much of the rest was tangled and inchoate. Yeats felt that he had to bring the book up to the standard and the spirit of his final period. That a book called *A Vision* should be subject to revision might seem absurd, though perhaps not more so than the idea mocked by Thomas Paine in *The Age of Reason,* of attributing two testaments to God. In revising it Yeats reconceived the book as a whole.

A Vision had begun in 1917 when, during their honeymoon, Mrs. Yeats sought to divert her husband from disquieting thoughts about having married the wrong woman by attempting automatic writing. Originally a marital stratagem, the automatic writing suddenly took off in startling new directions. It offered, in fragments, a symbology far more complicated that any Yeats had come to on his own, and yet it roughly jibed with his previous ideas. The manner of the revelation was somewhat embarrassing: it was one thing to be a mystic, and another to be a mystic's consort. Mrs. Yeats had no wish to be presented to the world as a Pythoness, and her husband could hardly claim to be his own oracle. Moreover, he felt that his readers would be put off by the idea of spooky communicators. So when he first brought out the book, instead of claiming authorship or joint authorship, he offered a little facade of mystery. The title page of the 1926 *Vision* read: *A Vision: An Explanation of Life Founded upon the Writings of Giraldus Cambrensis and upon Certain Theories Attributed to Kusta Ben Luka.* Needless to say, neither of these worthies had anything to do with the book. Yet it would have been hard for a reader to know for certain whether Yeats was fooling or not, or why he should wish to dissimulate.

For the second edition he resolved to tell the true story of how the book came into being. Mrs. Yeats said to me that this decision provoked the most painful quarrel, perhaps the only serious one, of their marriage. She wanted him to publish the book straight-forwardly, without explanation or preliminaries. But Yeats evidently felt that to do so would be to promulgate the Tables of the Law without the necessary preliminary of ascending Mount Sinai.

44

Yeats about 1905

Besides, the actual origin of the book was as fabulous as any concocted claim of Giraldus's or Kusta's help.

So in the 1937 edition Yeats owned up publicly to his domestic Delphi. The fact that the book had developed out of his marriage bed gave it that blend of love, beauty, and wisdom which he had always sought. He also reconceived its character. It was not a new religion, it was not a philosophy; it was a symbological myth. "One can believe in a myth," Yeats said; "one can only assent to a philosophy." Believing in his own myth did not come quite so easy as that, however. Yeats pondered this question and as early as 1928 had composed what he called "A Packet for Ezra Pound," which was a kind of dedication of the book to the man who would be least likely to accept it. The first *Vision* had been dedicated to a fellow-occultist, the second was packeted to a skeptic. The use of Pound was appropriate because, if Yeats could make his book seem sensible to someone of a different school of thought, he might speak with greater authority. It had occurred to him that the structural scheme of the *Cantos*, which he had heard Pound explain at Rapallo, bore at least some resemblance to his own structural scheme in *A Vision*. Coming from different ends of the intellectual scene, the two poets had unwittingly found common ground. Yeats concluded the "Packet for Ezra Pound" with four extraordinary sentences:

Some will ask whether I believe in the actual existence of my circuits of sun and moon. Those that include, now all recorded time in one circuit, now what Blake called "the pulsation of an artery," are plainly symbolical, but what of those that fixed, like the butterfly upon a pin, to our central date, the first day of our Era, divide actual history into periods of equal length? To such a question I can but answer that if sometimes, overwhelmed by miracle as all men must be when in the midst of it, I have taken such periods literally, my reason has soon recovered; and now that the system stands out clearly in my imagination I regard them as stylistic arrangements of experience comparable to the cubes in the drawing of Wyndham Lewis and to the ovoids in the sculpture of Brancusi. They have helped me to hold in a single thought reality and justice.

Only reality and justice! When Yeats began the paragraph, he seemed about to make a modest disclaimer of literal truth and of

46

preternatural assistance, but as he went along, he began to insist that the *Vision* had come to him miraculously, and at the end, in a sentence rewritten in his final period, he claims more than literal truth, he claims to have gathered together reality and justice. What appeared to be a partial retraction turned into an even more extravagant claim.

∾

Still, Yeats did not dash immediately from "A Packet for Ezra Pound" into the system itself. He must have felt that it would come all too suddenly upon readers not disposed to accept it, so he added a section, "Stories of Michael Robartes and His Friends," to predispose them in his favor. He had pretended that Giraldus and Kusta were actual sources, which they were not; the new stories of Robartes were not presented as anything but extravaganzas. One, which involved cuckoos and cuckolding, had been written in 1928. But the other, written in his last period, was closer to his feelings after the Steinach operation. It was based on something that had happened in Oxford in the early 1920s. As he informed Dorothy Wellesley on July 26, 1936, "We let our house in the Broad, Oxford, to some American girl students. In the middle of the night Alan Porter (later editor or sub-editor of *The Spectator*) climbed through the window. He was welcomed but found to be impotent. He explained that he had a great friend and when that friend had tired of a girl [he] had always taken her for himself. If he found a girl for himself he was impotent. The student said fetch your friend. He did. And after that all went well…I have worked it up into a charming fantasy of shyness. If the girl lay with the friend he felt she belonged to the family: once was enough."

Impotence was clearly a great subject for Yeats, even during his second puberty. In *A Vision* he has this story told by the young woman who calls herself Denise de l'Isle Adam, as something that has happened to her. The absurd name she bears is of course based upon that of Villiers de l'Isle Adam, the author of the symbolist drama *Axël,* which fascinated Yeats as a young man. In that play, Axël, on the ground that life cannot possibly live up to their hopes for it, persuades the heroine to die with him at once rather than consummate their love and experience inevitable disappointment. In Yeats's idealistic youth, this antiphysical play had meant a good deal to him, and in his own play *The Shadowy Waters,* the lovers behave rather similarly. But Denise, in the course of recounting her own experience, comments that Axël in Villiers' play was motivated not by scorn of life and sexuality but by shyness and temporary impotence. This is a worldly-wise revision of the solemnity of *Axël,* in keeping with Yeats's later manner and outlook. And yet the story is not merely one of corporeal accommodation. It implies something else, that Denise loves one man with her soul and accepts the other with her body. The soul may keep its distance while the body embraces, and vice versa. The same theme animates Yeats's late group of poems, "The Three Bushes," where the mistress is averse to physical but not to spiritual love and asks her serving maid to substitute covertly for her in the dark with her lover, while she loves him spiritually in the light. The maid, however, loves him body and soul. So this bawdy tale of mistress and maid had its metaphysical side, as in fact all sexuality has for Yeats from the beginning to end, with the body usually proving the soul's power.

When it came to the avowedly mystical materials of *A Vision,* Yeats left alone the sections of the first *Vision* that dealt with psychology and with cultural history, only omitting an indiscreet prophecy of the immediate future. He concentrated his revision upon the sections that dealt with the metaphysical aspect of the self and with the afterlife. These sections had originally been full of admissions of uncertainty, which Yeats now largely deleted. He set a more confident tone, and made much more frequent resort to metaphors. But in a way these sections could never be finished. The more he refined them, the more he came up against central problems that he could not solve without pretending to more certainty than he had. The principal ones were the relation of the human self to its spiritual counterpart, a sort of ethereal alter ego, and the battle between free will and determinism. In response to the first, Yeats had a theory about the spirits, which he expressed most fully in a note called "Seven Propositions," never published by him. The first proposition holds that "Reality is a timeless and

W. B. Yeats with his family in the 1920s

spaceless community of Spirits which perceive each other. Each Spirit is determined by and determines those it perceives, and each Spirit is unique." The second states, "When these Spirits reflect themselves in time and space they still determine each other, and each Spirit sees the others as thoughts, images, objects of sense. Time and space are unreal."

The obvious difficulty with these two propositions, and with the five others that I shall not rehearse, is that, if the Spirits alone are real, human beings have only a provisional, precarious existence. In other words, Yeats was reversing our usual assumption that spirits are shadowy creatures, human beings substantial ones, and instead making men and women shadowy and the spirits substantial. Much of Yeats's verse had tried to body forth the spirit world and spiritualize the natural one. But it was always couched in such a way that it could be taken as extravagant metaphor, emotionally warranted rather than doctrinally justified. He could not quite concede to flesh and blood the minor role which his theory seemed to accord them. As a result, he not only limited the autonomy of the spirits in *A Vision,* but in the verse written at the same time he suggested that the spirits were jealous of the human and longed to be bodied so as to undergo "desecration and the lover's night." In his early verse the fairies kidnap human children out of the same jealousy of the mortal condition, and the gods—Celtic or Greek—fall in love with them and rape or seduce them.

The second problem in the book, free will as opposed to determinism, Yeats also left open. So though *A Vision* has the semblance of a deterministic system, in which past and future obey mechanical laws and beings occupy their allotted and fixed places on a wheel, Yeats—once he had perfected the system—gave play to what he called the Thirteenth Cone or Sphere, a kind of god-surrogate who can alter everything. By introducing the unpredictable into a system predicated on predictability, Yeats kept the relation of physical and metaphysical forever wavering. So these two great issues—of spirit and substance, of freedom and compulsion—were left as blurred in the second *Vision* as they had been in the first. Yeats refused to close the system. He did not mind that there were loose ends in it. The editor who dealt with the book for the Macmillan Company, Thomas Mark, once told me (and bound me to secrecy) that he had pointed out to Yeats some small inconsistencies in *A Vision;* to his surprise Yeats showed no special concern. It was as if he knew that the symbology would always be imperfect.

৶

After the publication of the second *Vision,* Yeats began to express some dissatisfaction with it. In "A General Introduction to My Work," he said that "subconscious preoccupation" with the theme of Unity of Being "brought me *A Vision,* its harsh geometry an incomplete interpretation." By this time, it was not Mrs. Yeats's subconscious, but Yeats's—she had been demoted to being simply an agent of his subconscious mind. "I don't know whether I want my friends to see it," he wrote. In a letter to Ethel Mannin he called *A Vision* his "public philosophy," and said he had a "private philosophy" as well. At one time *A Vision* had been private, but now it was merely exoteric, and there were ideas far more intimate that he had not revealed. His private philosophy, he informed Ethel Mannin, was "the material dealing with individual mind which came to me with that on which the mainly historical *Vision* is based. I have not published it because I only half understand it."

I think we can surmise at least some of the topics that Yeats's private philosophy included. So we might shadow forth still another vision, a third one, the one he never wrote down. This one seems to underlie all his work, but only as he reached the end of his life did he fully acknowledge it. More than ever before he recognized certain problems as having more than one solution, and thought his best course must be to register rather than resolve his conflicting responses to them.

What could dissatisfy him about *A Vision* was not so much its incoherence upon ultimate matters as its sanguine air. The eternal round goes on, "birth is heaped on birth," the soul undergoes its appointed metamorphoses; all seems neat and ongoing. In one section Yeats rebukes Paul Valéry for having rejoiced, in *Le Cimetiere marin,* that all life must pass. No, he says, he prefers to remember a young woman (Maud Gonne's daughter Iseult) who sang on a Normandy beach a song of her own composition in which each verse ended, "O Lord, let something remain." Yet Yeats was not always so life-affirming. In his own poem "Vacillation," he imagined a Chinese warlord saying to battleweary men, "Let all things pass away." Desire is balanced by scornful renunciation. If *A Vision* had no place for such sentiments, that was one of its shortcomings.

Yeats explicitly acknowledged that one subject he had neglected in *A Vision* was what he called "the beatific vision." In a way this was the cornerstone of the whole system, because the point of almost endless becoming is to achieve at last true unified being. Had Yeats written in his prose book what he expressed in his verse, he would have discoursed on the several forms that beatitude may take: there is the unity of lovers, achieved by a communion of minds and bodies; there is the positive unity achieved by heroes at the culmination of their exploits, and the negative unity achieved by saints at the culmination of their sufferings; there is the unity that souls may achieve after death; there is the unity achieved by works of art out of gross matter; and there is another unity, a more unassuming one, which sometimes steals upon us unawares in casual circumstances, not less momentous for being unsought. Each of these states defied and transcended the usual condition of life. That condition Yeats always framed as a conflict of contraries.

But the beatific vision could be only one end of the seesaw. The other was its obverse, a vision which nullified all that the beatific vision offered. Instead of completeness, there was blankness. Instead of enterprise, there was futility. In his youth Yeats had envisaged the coming of the rose as a benign renaissance, but he had also envisaged the coming of malign destruction in "The Valley of the Black Pig." In his later work, though he never forsook the idea of renaissance completely, his prophecies had often an element of terror. The avatar of "The Second Coming" is a fearful medley of man and beast, and slouches towards Bethlehem as a symbol of the Antichrist who will destroy all that has been

W. B. Yeats with his wife in Rapallo after suffering from Malta fever, about 1928

begotten. Threats of God burning time, or of the poet setting a match to the time world because it failed to measure up to his standard for it, had always provided a negative undertone in Yeats's generally affirming verse. His conception of the afterlife offered a comparable doubleness. In "The Cold Heaven," souls are punished with injustice instead of justice, heaven becomes hell. This poem was the opposite of a late poem such as "John Kinsella's Lament for Mistress Mary Moore," where we are told of heaven, "No expectation fails there, / No pleasing habit ends." The afterlife might or might not be benign.

When Yeats considered love from the obverse point of view it no longer stood as a symbol of completeness but as a locked relationship of torturer and victim, of love and hate. So "Her Vision in the Wood" is much closer to Baudelaire than to Dante, and in a late poem Yeats speaks of hatred of God as a sentiment just as inspiring as love of God.

His attitude towards art had also two aspects. Long ago, in 1925, he had written in "Sailing to Byzantium" of the longing of an old man to break out of detested nature and into the perfection of art. His friend Sturge Moore reminded him that art is itself natural, and Yeats agreed by writing his second poem, "Byzantium," in which also the emphasis comes upon the wonderful transformation which art effects upon life's images. But in his final period Yeats took up the subject again, in "The Circus Animals' Desertion." This time he put Byzantium aside, as if to deal with the problem more directly. He began by convoking his own earlier artistic images and pointed out that they had their origin in sexual passion but took on gradually an independent life. It might seem that this poem, like those about Byzantium, was to celebrate the purifying and distancing power of art. But in the last stanza Yeats suddenly turns around and declares:

> Those masterful images because complete
> Grew in pure mind, but out of what began?
> A mound of refuse or the sweepings of a street,
> Old kettles, old bottles, and a broken can,
> Old iron, old bones, old rags, that raving slut
> Who keeps the till. Now that my ladder's gone,

> I must lie down where all the ladders start,
> In the foul rag-and-bone shop of the heart.

Vaunt its mastery as it will, art must depend from the welter of unpurified experience, and that crude welter, like "the frog-spawn of a blind man's ditch"—his image for life in "A Dialogue of Self and Soul"—grips us again with its detestable fascination.

"The Circus Animals' Desertion" deals with the genesis of art but does not question its authority. It remains for another late poem of Yeats, "What Then?," to do that. In "What Then?" the old man surveys a life of high literary achievement:

> "The work is done," grown old he thought,
> "According to my boyish plan;
> Let the fools rage, I swerved in naught,
> Something to perfection brought"...

Plato's ghost, who has raised his quizzical cry, "What then?," after each stanza, sings it more insistently this time. "But louder sang that ghost, 'What then?'" The seeming victories of art over time may be as meaningless as any other illusion.

What Yeats questions in art he also questions in life. Usually he praised life, though often grudgingly or defiantly. But there were moments when he could see, obversely, an ultimate emptiness. His late poem "Meru" is one of the most telling expressions of this idea:

> Civilisation is hooped together, brought
> Under a rule, under the semblance of peace
> By manifold illusion; but man's life is thought,
> And he, despite his terror, cannot cease
> Ravening through century after century,
> Ravening, raging, and uprooting that he may come
> Into the desolation of reality.

Beatifically, reality is where "all the barrel hoops are knit," according to Yeats's poem "There," but obversely, as in "Meru," the hoops will not hold, and what we have is "desolation." "Egypt and Greece, good-bye, and good-bye, Rome!" is the splendid dismissal

W. B. Yeats telling a joke, sometime in the 1930s

of the pretensions of civilizations to escape from nothingness. In "Meru" Yeats attributes this recognition to the East, and in another late poem, "The Statues," declares, "Grimalkin crawls to Buddha's emptiness" (that is, a worshipper who is nothing crawls to a god who is nothing, too). The East is a hemisphere of his own mind as well as a geographical entity. In "The Black Tower," Yeats evokes the tower which he had used often before with all kinds of iconic meanings, but this time the terrible possibility of its meaninglessness appears even to its defenders. "The Pilgrim" in a poem of that name has fasted, made the pilgrimage to Lough Derg, questioned the dead, and now summarizes all that he has learned as "fol de rol de rolly O"—meaninglessness with a lilt.

This obverse vision makes itself felt in Yeats's last poems perhaps most notably in regard to death. As befitted a man grown old, the poems are full of the dead, the dying, the about to die. His son recalls that the doctors had given Yeats only three years to live, and that he had told his wife, "I am disgracing the family by dying so young." The subject had often beset him earlier. Twenty years before, in a group of poems about Aubrey Beardsley's sister Mabel, Yeats had praised those who laugh "into the face of death." In "Lapis Lazuli," which comes in his final volume, he describes the death of various tragic heroes, especially Hamlet and Lear, and attributes to them not exactly laughter but a sort of tragic gaiety. (He does the same in his prose work *On the Boiler*.) The actors who play Hamlet and Lear are right in not weeping at the moment of their stage deaths, because Hamlet and Lear have expressed fundamental energies and these, as Blake said and Yeats quoted, are "eternal delight." Another way of putting this would be that they complete their images of themselves at the very moment that death strikes: "Blackout: Heaven blazing into the head." Yeats liked to talk of a Norse god who died as a sacrifice to himself. Tragic heroes, in pursuing their destiny to its end, make death their accomplice rather than their adversary.

Against this view of death as a means of tragic illumination, joyfully received, which many of his poems uphold, there is an obverse view that it may be nothing of the sort. Occasionally Yeats expresses this. If in "Under Ben Bulben" Yeats could assure his readers that death is only a momentary interruption before the soul is again reincarnated, he offers no such consolation in another poem, "The Apparitions." Here the refrain, based as Mrs. Yeats told me upon an actual nightmare of Yeats's which he interpreted to be about death, only repeats,

> Fifteen apparitions have I seen;
> The worst a coat upon a coat-hanger.

Perhaps the gloomiest of all Yeats's poems is the very late one "The Man and the Echo." Like a number of his other poems, it is a debate, but this time the adversary is not self nor soul nor heart nor antiself, but a hollow and defeatist echo. It begins with the man remorsefully reviewing things he has misdone or failed to do:

> And all seems evil until I
> Sleepless would lie down and die.

To which Echo responds without pity,

> Lie down and die.

But the man refuses to accept this solution. He is full of humanistic affirmation:

> That were to shirk
> The spiritual intellect's great work . . .
> While man can still his body keep
> Wine or love drugs him to sleep . . .
> But body gone he sleeps no more,
> And till his intellect grows sure
> That all's arranged in one clear view,
> Pursues the thoughts that I pursue,
> Then stands in judgment on his soul,
> And, all work done, dismisses all
> Out of intellect and sight
> And sinks at last into the night.

W. B. Yeats with Edith Shackleton Heald, the last of Yeats's beloveds, and Mrs. Edmund Dulac (seated right), about 1938

To which Echo answers only,

> Into the night.

In desperation at this blankness, the man cries,

> O Rocky Voice,
> Shall we in that great night rejoice?

In these lines Yeats recalls the first poem in his final volume, "The Gyres," in which he had declared,

> Out of cavern comes a voice
> And all it knows is that one word, "Rejoice!"

But in "The Man and the Echo," the man answers his almost hopeless question with an even more hopeless one, still addressed to Echo:

> What do we know but that we face
> One another in this place?

This time Echo does not have to answer. To the obverse vision, any idea that life and afterlife make sense cannot be sustained. So Yeats, who had claimed at the end of "A Packet" to hold in a single thought reality and justice, was obliged by his inner honesty to allow for the possibility that reality was desolation and justice a figment.

Mrs. Yeats told me that it would have taken her husband a hundred years to complete his work. I surmise that he was roughening the edges of the two forces he had always seen at work in the world, the one looking askance at reality as something temporary, provisional, and tidal, the other regarding it as hive- or nest-like, tenacious, lasting. In May 1938 he dictated but never published a

W. B. Yeats in the 1930s

quatrain in which the first line questioned, "What is the explanation of it all?" and the following lines went on,

> What does it look like to a learned man?
> Nothings in nothings whirled, or when he will,
> From nowhere into nowhere nothings run.

Perhaps in no other poem did Yeats take the obverse of the beatific vision so darkly. But the word *nothing* resounds in two of his late plays: the old man in *Purgatory* says at the end, "Twice a murderer and all for nothing," and the last speech of *The Herne's Egg* memorializes blankness, "All that trouble and nothing to show for it..." Long before Yeats had written, "Where there is nothing, there is God," but he had also had King Fergus say, "Now I have grown nothing, knowing all." In "The Gyres," Yeats indicated that out of any "rich dark nothing" the whole gazebo could be built up once again. He could conceive of nothing as empty and also as pregnant. I think he saw with increasing sharpness the clash between the urge to have done with fine distinctions, subtle passions, and differentiated matter, and the urge to keep them at all costs. In his last play, *The Death of Cuchulain,* the final chorus asks,

> Are those things that men adore and loathe
> Their sole reality?

As Yeats reached his life's end, he recognized that he would never be able to decide between the beatific vision and its obverse. The image of life as cornucopia was relentlessly undermined by the image of life as an empty shell. In his last play he allows the central characters to share in this sense of the indeterminable. The old man in *Purgatory* thinks that he can release his mother's soul from purgatory by killing his son, only to discover that his ghastly deed has no effect. This play has been read as an elegy upon the decline of the Irish country house, but I think it should be read primarily as a lament for the impossibility of imposing the beatific vision upon its horrid obverse. The Steinach operation symbolized for Yeats his attempt to impose potency upon impotence, yet even as he claimed to be young he knew he was not. Pain and nullification accompanied him during the years that he lived out his second puberty. At the end we must, as he once said, "sing amid our uncertainty." In his youth he predicted in "The Man Who Dreamed of Faeryland" that one day God would "burn nature with a kiss." In a late letter he returned to this idea: "The last kiss is given to the void." The artist imposes form upon the void but knows that the void may yet overwhelm. In the fiery furnaces where universes are made they may also go to die. "The painter's brush consumes his dreams," Yeats wrote, and knew that the poet's pen belongs similarly to a process of decreation as much as of creation. A last letter of Yeats took comfort in one thing alone, that man if he cannot know the truth can at last embody it. Not without unconscious pride, he said he would embody it in the completion of his life. What he meant was that the great questions could be given only momentary answers, couched in passionate utterance. Visionaries or not, we are only, as Falstaff says, "mortal men, mortal men."

James Joyce by Brancusi, 1929

James Joyce
In and Out of Art

JAMES JOYCE thought about his centenary, recently celebrated, long before it occurred to his readers to do so. He scrawled in a notebook on Bloomsday, the day of *Ulysses,* in 1924, "Today 16 of June 20 years after. Will anybody remember this date." His Stephen Dedalus in *Ulysses* asks the same question as he jots down lines for a new poem, "Who ever anywhere will read these written words?" Stephen also recalls, with a twinge, how before leaving for Paris he gave instructions that in the event of his death his epiphanies should be deposited in all the major libraries of the world, *including Alexandria:* "Someone was to read them there after a few thousand years..." The library at Alexandria having been burned centuries before, chances were slim that anyone would be reading his epiphanies there at any time. Still, if Joyce mocked such immortal longings, it was because he had immortal longings to mock. His brother Stanislaus, who drew a sharp line between fiction and fact, remembered that James had given him similar instructions for the disposal of his poems and epiphanies before leaving for Paris in 1902. No one will object to brave youths displaying youthful bravado. Flushed with talent or its semblance, they have all claimed with Shakespeare:

> Not marble, nor the gided monuments
> Of princes, shall outlive this powerful rhyme.

Sometimes they've been right.

Joyce was convinced that a great future lay in store for him, and on the promise of it he allowed people to help him secure it. In 1904 he thought briefly that the moment had arrived; an Irish-American millionaire named Kelly seemed about to lend him money to start up a weekly magazine which was to be called *The Goblin.* Joyce said to his friend Francis Sheehy Skeffington, who was to be coeditor, "I think I am coming into my kingdom." Unfortunately, millionaire Kelly withdrew. Eight years later the same phrase occurs in a letter from Joyce to his wife: "I hope that the day may come when I shall be able to give you the fame of being beside me when I have entered into my Kingdom." That he was still borrowing "left right and centre" did not dishearten him. In 1907 his second child was born in a paupers' ward, but in that atmosphere Joyce confided to his brother, "My mind is of a type superior to and more civilized than any I have met up to the present." An empty wallet did not diminish his conviction of spiritual affluence. His confidence persisted as he grew older, and his putative kingdom continued to include the posterity for whom he thought his books would be required texts. When Max Eastman asked him why he was writing *Finnegans Wake* in the way he was, Joyce replied, with a brag intended to provoke a smile, "To keep the critics busy for three hundred years."

The first hundred of these three hundred years Joyce appears to have weathered quite well. His books are indeed studied all over the world and have their effect even on those who do not read them. If nothing else, writers in England as elsewhere have to choose when they start a novel whether or not to be traditional, whereas in the pre-Joycian past they could be traditional without scruple. Joyce does not lack for admirers; he does not lack for detractors either. His detractors are repelled by the Joyce fans who obsessively follow Leopold Bloom's trail around Dublin, or climb the stairs of the martello tower at Sandycove, or drink at the much refurbished Davy Byrne's. Still, such activities are not more pernicious, or cultic, than climbing Wordsworth's Helvellyn, or visiting Hawthorne's House of the Seven Gables in Salem or Proust's aunt's house in Illiers. If Joyce particularly inspires such pilgrimages, it is perhaps because we long to be on closer terms with this

Sketch of Joyce by John Yeats, evidently done at the Abbey Theatre in October 1902

scriptor absconditus, this indrawn writer, in the hope of achieving an intimacy with him which he does not readily afford.

Another reason for seeing the places described in his books is that Joyce, although he transformed those places into words, did not invent them. He said, "He is a very bold man who dares to alter in the presentment, still more to deform whatever he has seen and heard" (May 5, 1906). This was in connection with the book *Dubliners.* He was always trying to verify details of the city which lay almost a thousand miles from the table at which he was writing about it. How many feet down was the area in front of the house at 7 Eccles Street? What kind of trees were there on Leahy's terrace? Some of Joyce's flavor comes as a reward for this zeal. For example, in *A Portrait of the Artist as a Young Man,* Stephen Dedalus, after protesting to the rector that he has been unjustly pandied, leaves the rector's room and walks down the long corridor. At the end of it he bumps his elbow against the door. I am told that generations of Clongowes pupils have bumped their elbows against this same door. Joyce attended so carefully to such minute particulars that he claimed, if Dublin were destroyed, the city could be reconstructed from his books. Its immortality would be assured through his. Other novelists are, however, much more likely to present a city in reconstructable form. Joyce offers no architectural information, only places to bump elbows, or to lean them, to see out of the corner of an eye, to recognize by a familiar smell. The city rises in bits, not in masses. Anything else would be travelogue.

He was at once dependent upon the real and superior to it. His attitude may be elicited from a story he once told to his French Academician friend Louis Gillet. It was about an old Blasket Islander who had lived on his island from birth and knew nothing about the mainland or its ways. But on one occasion he did venture over and in a bazaar found a small mirror, something he had never seen in his life. He bought it, fondled it, gazed at it, and as he rowed back to the Blaskets he took it out of his pocket, stared at it some more, and murmured, "Oh Papa! Papa!" He jealously guarded the precious object from his wife's eye, but she observed that he was hiding something and became suspicious. One hot day, when both were at work in the fields, he hung his jacket on a hedge. She saw her chance, rushed to it, and extracted from a pocket the object her husband had kept so secret. But when she looked in the mirror, she cried, "Ach, it's nothing but an old woman!" and angrily threw it down so that it broke against a stone. For Joyce the story had many implications, such as that man was filial and woman was vain. But the main one was that a mirror held up to nature will reflect the holder's consciousness as much as what is reflected. He could quote with approval (May 16, 1907) Pater's remark, "Art is life seen through a temperament."

When Joyce was young so many subjects pressed urgently upon him that he had only to choose among them. As he grew older he needed more hints. He sometimes thought he must alter his quiet life so as to secure them. Of course he could say defensively to Djuna Barnes, "[Johann Sebastian] Bach led a very uneventful life," but when he was with Ernest Hemingway he discussed the possibility of going to Africa. Mrs. Joyce encouraged him: "Jim can do with a spot of lion hunting," she said. "The thing we must face," said Joyce, whose sight was bad, "is that I couldn't see the lion." His wife was not to be silenced: "Hemingway'd describe him to you and afterwards you could go up to him and touch him and smell him. That's all you'd need." But the material he needed lay closer to home. For the main theme of *Ulysses* and of his play *Exiles,* Joyce could rely on an incident which did not happen but which he briefly thought had happened. A onetime friend claimed in 1909 that Nora Barnacle, in the days when Joyce was courting her, had shared her favors with himself. But when Joyce was actually writing his novel and play five years later, he had trouble reactivating the jealousy he had once felt so intensely. His wife complained to their friend Frank Budgen, "Jim wants me to go with other men so that he will have something to write about." She seems to have failed him in this wifely duty. She did however oblige him to the extent of beginning a letter to him with the words, "Dear Cuckold," with the helpful aim of sharpening his pen for *Ulysses.*

James Joyce, 1919

Joyce for his part made comparable sacrifices for his art. In 1917 and 1918 he was beginning to write the Nausicaa episode of *Ulysses,* in which Bloom ogles a girl named Gerty MacDowell on the beach. Joyce seems to have felt that he must do something similar. He made overtures to two women, perhaps with his book ulteriorly in mind. The first occurred in Locarno, where he went for a time to enjoy a milder climate than Zurich's. In 1917 a woman doctor—one of the first women doctors in Germany—named Gertrud Kaempffer was staying above Locarno, in Orselina, recovering from tuberculosis after having nearly died of that disease. Joyce, afflicted with serious eye trouble, was living in Locarno itself at the Pension Daheim. One evening Gertrud Kaempffer came down by funicular railway to visit some friends of hers in the same pension. They introduced her to Joyce, who because of his three published books and his obvious intellectual distinction had a certain local celebrity. He took an immediate interest in the young doctor, and after some talk offered to see her to the funicular. But her friends whispered to her that Mrs. Joyce would be jealous, so Dr. Kaempffer declined.

They happened to meet next day, however, in front of the spa hotel near the casino. After some conversation Joyce walked part of the way home with her. When she offered her hand in parting, he held it in his hands for a moment, stroked it, and told her how fond he was of such delicate skin, of such fine, slender hands. (She considered her hands to be only thin and sickly.) Gerty MacDowell —the object of Bloom's prurient scrutiny—has a similar "waxen pallor" and, as we are told, "Her hands were of finely veined alabaster with tapering fingers and as white as lemon juice and queen of ointments could make them though it was not true that she used to wear kid gloves in bed or take a milk footbath either." Joyce lent Gertrud Kaempffer *A Portrait of the Artist as a Young Man.* She was interested and asked his help with certain English words which she did not understand. Joyce probably assumed that as a doctor she had much knowledge of the world. In fact during her medical course her fellow students and professors had cosseted her, as one of the first women students, and at the end of it she fell ill; so she was inexperienced and rather startled by the sexual overtures which Joyce soon made. She was fascinated by his

71

mind, he indifferent, as she felt, to hers. When she would not accede he asked her to correspond with him, and to use for the purpose the poste restante in Zurich. (Bloom also uses the poste restante in his clandestine correspondence with Martha Clifford.) Dr. Kaempffer reluctantly said no; she was put off by the idea of exchanging letters in secret.

Still, he occupied her thoughts, and she opened with interest the two letters he sent to her. Molly Bloom recalls how Bloom "wrote me that letter with all those words in it," and in *A Portrait of the Artist* Joyce depicts Stephen Dedalus's writing obscene letters and leaving them about in the hope that some girl will find them. With Gertrud Kaempffer Joyce indulged a kindred proclivity. Like Stephen's their correspondence seemed to be outside space and time, though it was not. He said he loved her and made clear that his love was physical. He hoped she had the same feelings. He said he wished to be entirely straightforward and to leave to her the decision about intimacy.

Then, perhaps to excite her as well as himself, he described in his fastidious handwriting his first sexual experience. It had occurred when he was fourteen. He was walking with the family nanny near some woods when she asked him to look the other way. He did so and heard the sound of liquid splashing on the ground. Joyce used the word *piss*, with which the young doctor was unfamiliar. The sound aroused him. "I jiggled furiously," he wrote. She did not understand this phrase either, and was later told by someone that it was a kind of Scottish dance. In *Finnegans Wake* the principal character, Earwicker, is accused of having performed the same act opposite two micturating girls: "Slander, let it lie its flattest, has never been able to convict our good and great and no ordinary...Earwicker, that homogenius man, as a pious author called him, of any graver impropriety than that...of having behaved with ongentilmensky immodus opposite a pair of dainty maid servants in the swoolth of the rushy hollow whither...dame nature in all innocence and spontaneously and about the same hour of the eventide sent them both..." Joyce evidently recognized a farcical shamefulness in his own behavior. He confided in one of his letters to Gertrud Kaempffer another frailty: he found it particularly provocative when lying with a woman, he said, to be afraid of being discovered.

Gertrud Kaempffer did not regard these sentiments as fetching, and perhaps they were written more to indulge Joyce's own fantasy than in the hope of sharing it with her. She tore up the letters, in case anyone should read them, and did not reply. They would not meet again until a year later when, on her way to visit friends in Zurich, she caught sight in a public place of an unhappy looking, emaciated man, and moved closer to see if it could be Joyce. He suddenly turned around, recognized her and greeted her warmly, and invited her to a café. She could not go, having an appointment. Might she not come to the hotel later for a drink? Foreseeing embarrassment, she refused again. Joyce looked pained, shook hands, and said goodbye. All that survived of this idyll was a recollection of having been aroused by a woman named Gertrud. At least he could draw one thing from it—the name of the young woman over whom Bloom excites himself in the Nausicaa episode—Gerty. As he had said in *Giacomo Joyce,* "Write it, damn you, write it! What else are you good for?"

He needed more hints for the episode than the aloof Dr. Kaempffer provided, and the second of his forays occurred some months after the first, this time in Zurich. One day in 1918 Joyce looked out of a window in his flat and happened to see, in a flat in the next building, a young woman pulling a toilet chain. It was an act that as we have observed had distinct erotic implications for him. He contrived to speak to this second young woman, whose name was Marthe Fleischmann, on the street. She had a limp, and he would give the same limp to Gerty MacDowell in the Nausicaa episode. He stared at her with amazement as if they had met before and was later to tell her that she looked exactly like a young woman he had seen many years earlier on the Dublin strand. Marthe Fleischmann seems to have coyly declined this gambit.

How far his feelings derived from the needs of his novel, and how far the novel from his amorous needs, were questions Joyce did not have to answer. As he had written his brother thirteen years before, "there cannot be any substitute for the individual passion as the motive power of everything—art and philosophy included" (February 7, 1905). Joyce kept watching for Marthe Fleischmann and she, far from ignoring his attentions, closed the shutters of her windows. He wrote her an ardent letter partly in French, in a disguised handwriting, marked especially by his use of Greek *e*'s.

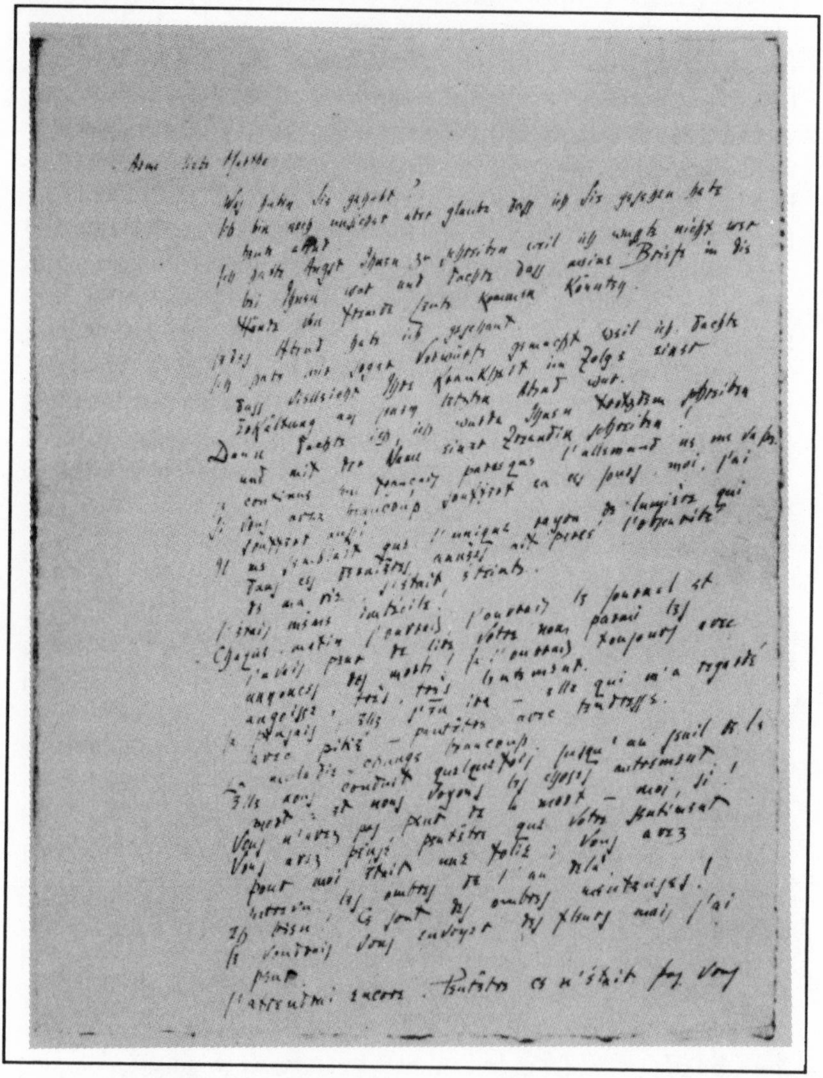

Letter from Joyce to Marthe Fleischmann, late January 1919

que j'ai vu ?

J'ai vu mon livre de poésies dans votre main.

Est-ce que vous l'avez compris ? votre ... — quelque ...

j'ai écrit quelque chose pourtant ... beaucoup mes amis

... très amer qui a blessé beaucoup mes amis

... j'ai souffert aussi !

Je désire encore ... de vous ... cette lettre ?

si elle tombe ... de votre ... propre ...

à Paris

Je veux jeter cette lettre à la boîte.

Je ne peux plus attendre !

g.

He would have Mrs. Yelverton Barry in *Ulysses* complain that Bloom wrote to her "an anonymous letter in prentice backhand full of indecent proposals," and would have Bloom use Greek *e*'s in corresponding with another Martha. Joyce begged Marthe to tell him her name. She will not mind if he suggests she is Jewish, for after all Jesus lay in the womb of a Jewish mother. As for himself, he is a writer and at a pivotal moment in his life. His age is the same as Dante's when he began the *Divine Comedy* and as Shakespeare's when he fell in love with the Dark Lady of the *Sonnets* (a date we don't know). He is supremely unhappy; he must see her.

Marthe yielded to these importunities and agreed to meet him—whether she was Jewish or not. When they met Joyce did not spend much time on religion; rather he turned the conversation to the congenial subject of women's drawers, always a titillating topic for him, and one which figures prominently in the Nausicaa episode. It was not easy for her to arrange because, as she archly confided, she had a "guardian" named Rudolf Hiltpold. Hiltpold was really her lover, the man who paid her rent. He was vigilant, and she had to be circumspect. Joyce inscribed a copy of *Chamber Music* to her and left it in her letterbox. It was an appropriate gift for Marthe, especially since he has Bloom in *Ulysses* reflect jokingly about the relation of chamber music to chamber pots. Evidently Marthe was impressed. Gerty MacDowell in the Nausicaa episode would also be interested in poetry, though of an even more hopeless kind.

Joyce now prepared a curious ceremony. On February 2, 1918, his thirty-sixth birthday, he arranged for her to have tea at the studio of his friend Frank Budgen. A note he sent to her that morning is headed "Marias Lichtmesse" or Candlemas, the feast commemorating the Purification of the Virgin Mary, which also takes place on February 20. He evidently wished to infuse a touch of mariolatry in his sexual approach, as in *Ulysses* he parallels Bloom's secular adoration of Gerty MacDowell with a men's retreat at a church dedicated to the Virgin. For the Zurich occasion Joyce borrowed a handsome Jewish silver candlestick such as is lighted during the festival of Chanukah and brought it to Frank Budgen's studio. He explained to the painter that Marthe would be arriving a little later.

Budgen had scruples about assisting his friend in this infidelity and said so. Joyce replied severely, "If I permitted myself any restraint in this matter it would be spiritual death to me." Rather than feel guilty of spiritual murder, Budgen gave in. There were further preparations. Budgen's paintings would do well enough as décor, except that there were no nudes among them. The painter had therefore to whip up on the spot a charcoal drawing of a voluptuous nude. Joyce said that in spite of his unwillingness to use given names, on this one occasion he and Budgen must call each other not Joyce and Budgen, but Jim and Frank, and use the intimate form *du,* because he had spoken so often of Budgen to Marthe that she would find strange any more formal style of address.

Marthe arrived for Candlemas and Chanukah. When candles are lighted on Candlemas the priest speaks of them as symbolizing the light which shall enlighten the Gentiles and also the glory of the people of Israel. This text seemed to give warrant to Joyce's syncretism. He lit the Jewish candlestick ostensibly so she could see the paintings better, actually to lend a Judaeo-Christian glimmer to the erotic rendezvous. He toured the paintings with her, and as Budgen recalled, won a reproachful smirk from Marthe when he called to her attention the fat nude. Eventually Joyce took her home. He met Budgen later that evening and confided, "I have explored the coldest and hottest parts of a woman's body." Gerty MacDowell reproaches Bloom, "you saw all the secrets of my bottom drawer." Such scientific lechery would be mocked in the Circe episode of *Ulysses.* Presumably the encounter remained exploratory, or so Budgen, knowing his friend's latent inhibitions, surmised. As for Marthe, she always referred to her acquaintance with Joyce as "eine Platonische Liebe." A day or two later Joyce was asked by another friend why he had borrowed the candlestick, and he replied, "For a black mass." Bloom, ruminating about Gerty, and at the same time remembering the words "Next year in Jerusalem" from still another Jewish festival, that of Passover, conflates the two in the Nausicaa episode by thinking how she "showed me her next year in drawers."

Further meetings with Marthe Fleischmann now became out of the question. The redoubtable "guardian" Rudolf Hiltpold got wind of the proceedings and wrote a threatening letter to Joyce. Joyce went at once to see him, assured him that nothing had happened, and gave him all Marthe's letters. Hiltpold was mollified. Still, Marthe's haughty, naughty beguilements helped Joyce to compose the Nausicaa episode, a point he confirmed by sending her a postcard with greetings to Nausicaa from Odysseus. Her limp, her coyness, her prattling about Platonic love, her responsiveness to his interest in drawers all went to furnish out Gerty MacDowell, whose first name and pallid hands had come to him from his earlier attraction to Gertrud Kaempffer. The assignation on the Virgin Mary's Candlemas, with Chanukah and Passover trimmings, would have its uses. His would-be infidelities had served his book, if not his peculiar life.

These two incidents give a sense of Joyce's seeking cues for *Ulysses* and, no doubt, for himself, by listening to songs of the Sirens. Still, closeness to life was not enough. Granted that he believed himself from earliest youth to be an artist, it was as an Irish artist that he wished to become known. To that extent he was and always would be a part of the national literary revival. Although he spoke of *Finnegans Wake* as a universal history, the universe is given a distinct Irish coloration, and in a way the whole book is an arabesque on the Irish ballad of that title. Similarly his first work, now lost, written when he was nine, was on the most Irish of subjects—the death of Charles Stewart Parnell. In his youth perhaps his most passionate literary enthusiasm was for James Clarence Mangan, whom he complimented as "The national poet of Ireland" and as one who (he said) "had the whole past of the country at the back of his head," an ideal he marked out for himself as well. "An Irish safety pin is more important to me than an English epic," he remarked. Yet it was not Ireland as it had been that attracted him, but Ireland as it might be. Joyce was affected by the talk of renaissance that was in the air, and in the earliest as well as the final version of *A Portrait of the Artist,* that is, in 1904 as in 1914, he ended by summoning in his imagination a new Irish nation.

The Irishness of his books was a distinguishing mark. *Dubliners,* he told his brother, was "a moral history of the life I knew" (May 5, 1907), and to his publisher Grant Richards he wrote, "My intention was to write a chapter of the moral history of my country." Joyce is often considered amoral; he regarded himself as a moralist. Stephen Dedalus concludes *A Portrait* with the words, "I go forth to encounter for the millionth time the reality of experience and to forge in the smithy of my soul the uncreated conscience of my race." Irony-hunters, who throng to Joyce studies, have been reluctant to take this expressed ambition of Stephen seriously. Joyce did so, however; in an earnest letter to his wife in 1912 he said, "I am one of the writers of this generation who are perhaps creating at last a conscience in the soul of this wretched race." His books move obliquely, even urbanely, toward this goal. In nine articles he wrote from 1907 to 1912 in a Triestine newspaper he presented his country's plight in more downright fashion. He offered these in 1914 to a publisher in Rome. They were not accepted: a pity, since they would have confirmed Joyce's "political awareness," a quality he valued in Turgenev. If he was not a nationalist of anyone else's school he was his own nationalist. His brother records a conversation they had in April 1907; Stanislaus argued against a free Ireland on the grounds that freedom would make it intolerable. "What the devil are your politics?" asked James. "Do you not think Ireland has a right to govern itself and is capable of doing so?" As an Irish writer, Joyce in 1912 went to the head of Sinn Féin, Arthur Griffith, to secure his help in having *Dubliners* issued by an Irish firm. Griffith, later to be Ireland's first president, was powerless to help but received him with respect.

As Irish artist, Joyce could be contemptuous toward his literary compatriots, whom he derided as serving lesser gods than his own. He was nevertheless modest before his own art. He had many of the self-doubts that are often attributed only to lesser writers. Though his first book was verse, he did not pride himself greatly on it and even denied to Padraic Colum in 1909 that he was a poet. Of course he did not like it when others agreed with his estimate; Ezra Pound was one of those who deeply offended him in the late 1920s by urging him to file his new poems in the family

Bible. Joyce published them anyway but hedged his claim for them by giving them the title of *Pomes Penyeach*. He considered lyricism to be a vital part of his revelation of himself in his art, yet he played down his lyrics like a man unwilling to risk all on that throw. He was sufficiently affected by the criticism of early parts of *Finnegans Wake* to consider turning the book over to James Stephens for completion. As to *Ulysses,* he said of it to Samuel Beckett, "I may have oversystematized *Ulysses,*" though in fact Joyce had a Dantean skill in making what was systematic appear entirely improvisatory.

While he was writing his first book, Joyce owned up to uncertainties about the works with which he hoped to make his name. Of *Dubliners* he said to his brother, "The stories seem to be indisputably well done, but, after all, perhaps many people could do them as well." His autobiographical novel awakened even more misgivings. He had composed about twenty chapters of it under the title *Stephen Hero* when he abruptly announced to Stanislaus that he was changing the book's scope and redoing the early parts because they were not well written. When he had revised them, he was still dissatisfied. He decided to change the book completely; instead of having sixty-three chapters, as once planned, it would have only five. He would omit all its first part, in which he dealt with Stephen before he started his schooling. Instead he would begin at school. The name of his hero, Dedalus, would be changed to Daly. Stanislaus roundly objected to all these changes. "Tell me," said his brother, "is the novel to be your puke or mine?" An even less savory metaphor of the literary art comes in *Finnegans Wake* when Shem is accused, this time by his brother, of concocting an encaustic ink out of his own urine and excrement, and writing on the only foolscap available, his own body.

The decision to make the book into five chapters was to stand. Otherwise, the new version pleased Joyce little better. On December 15, 1907, he complained to Stanislaus, "The book begins at a railway station like most college stories; there are three companions in it, and a sister who dies by way of pathos. It is the old bag of tricks and a good critic would probably show that I am still struggling even in my stories with the stock figures discarded in Europe half a century ago." Stanislaus labored to reassure him. After all, there were not three companions, he said, but five. Sister Isabel died in the book because their brother Georgie had died in actual fact. Joyce conceded, "I didn't consciously use stock figures, but I fear that my mind, when I begin to write, runs in the groove of what I have read." This statement, recorded by Stanislaus, is the best hint we have that Joyce was determined to emerge from that groove, to stand literature on its head. He did just that, and evidently he intended it from the start.

These remarks prefigure the revisions he now made in *A Portrait of the Artist as a Young Man*. He eliminated sister Isabel from the book. No pathos, then. The opening scene at the railway station, evidently one in which Stephen arrives at Clongowes Wood College, is also left out. Joyce did not expunge Stephen's preschool days entirely, but he condensed them into three or four pages. The picture of infant consciousness, with shapes and touches and smells all distinct if not yet understood, and with words beginning to reverberate, was so astonishing as to provide William Faulkner with the technique for the equally admirable portrait of an idiot's mind in *The Sound and the Fury*. After this overture we might expect Joyce to take up the narrative in a sequential way, but there are telltale signs that he is not doing so. We gradually realize that Stephen has a fever, and that what we have been reading is not a history but a deliberate hodgepodge of memories of his earlier school days and holidays at home, rendered with the discontinuity and intensity appropriate to fever. Not until two-thirds of the way through the first chapter does Joyce change the tense, and when he does so he is signalizing not only Stephen's recovery from fever, but Stephen's apprehension of his own separateness as a recording consciousness. In *Ulysses* Joyce employs a somewhat comparable method by having Stephen recall the last two years of his life in a kind of fit, not of fever this time but of remorse.

Although his own life provided him with much material, he ruthlessly departed from it where he needed. The first chapter culminates with Stephen, unjustly pandied by Father Dolan, protesting to the rector. We know from Joyce's autobiographical recollections to Herbert Gorman that this incident was based upon fact. But this was by no means the only punishment Joyce received at Clongowes. The Punishment Book from that time is incomplete, but its surviving pages disclose no less than three other transgressions by Joyce in February and March 1889, at which time he was still only seven years old. He was given two pandies in February for not bringing a book to class, six in March for muddy boots, and four the same month for "vulgar language," an offense he would commit with growing frequency for the rest of his life. Since these three punishments were presumably meted out with just cause, Joyce ignored them and dealt only with the great injustice inflicted by Father Dolan. So Stephen became a victim, and a heroic one whose protest against unjust pandying at a Jesuit school could be a prelude to his larger protests in youth against Church and State.

During the year 1907 Joyce hesitated over keeping the name of Dedalus for his hero. If he changed it to Daly, he could write the book on the same realistic level as his epiphanies and stories of Dublin life. Call him Dedalus, and he would have to justify the oddity of this name for an Irishman; he would be able to do so only by connecting the contemporary character with the mythical artificer of wings and labyrinth. Some years later Joyce would speak of his art as "extravagant excursions into forbidden territory," and in choosing Dedalus over Daly he made such an excursion. In the last two chapters, instead of describing Stephen's movement outward from Ireland, Joyce represents also another movement, downward into myth. On a superficial level Stephen is dissociating himself; on a deeper level he is achieving an association with the Greek Daedalus, he is becoming himself a creature of myth. This decision led Joyce on to *Ulysses*. When asked why he had used the *Odyssey* so prominently in that book, Joyce replied, "It is my system of working." The method was established in 1907, when he threw Stephen Daly out and invited Stephen Dedalus in.

After he completed *A Portrait of the Artist as a Young Man,* Joyce had pretty well exhausted the possibilities of the artist-hero. For his next book he needed a new impluse. He was beginning to find it long before he used it, in 1907 also. In that year his remarks to his brother indicate that he was situating himself in relation to Ibsen, a figure he had idolized in his youth. "Auld Aibsen always wrote like a gentleman," he said, and added that he would himself not write so. On May 16, 1907, he commented, "Life is not so simple as Ibsen represents it. Mrs. Alving, for instance, is Mother-hood and so on ... It's all very fine and large, of course. If it had been writen at the time of Moses, we'd now think it wonderful. But it has no importance at this age of the world. It is a remnant of heroics, too." Joyce was very much opposed to heroics. "For me," he went on, "youth and motherhood are these two beside us." He pointed to a drunken boy of about twenty, a laborer, who had brought his mother into the trattoria where Joyce and Stanislaus were talking, while the mother was leading him home. The boy was hardly able to speak but was expressing his contempt for someone as well as he could. "I would like to put on paper the thousand complexities in his mind..." Joyce was evidently imagin-ing the dense consciousness that he would give to his characters in *Ulysses.* He went on, "Absolute realism is impossible, of course. That we all know ... But it's quite enough that Ibsen has omitted *all* question of finance from his thirteen dramas." Stanislaus took it upon himself to object, "Maybe there are some people who are not so preoccupied about money as you are." "Maybe so, by God," said his brother, "but I'd like to take twenty-five lessons from one of those chaps."

Given a writer so convinced that old ways would not do for him, *Ulysses* was from the start designed to break with precedents. "The task I set myself technically in writing a book from eighteen different points of view and in as many styles, all apparently unknown or undiscovered by my fellow tradesmen, that and the nature of the legend chosen would be enough to upset anyone's mental balance," Joyce (whose mental balance was not upset) confided to Harriet Weaver. In this book he set himself as many difficulties as he could, knowing that his genius would be equal to them. There is the title itself, so abrupt in its insistence on a mythical background, which however is never mentioned as it was in *A Portrait of the Artist*. The author's silence about it is intimidating, yet the relation to the *Odyssey* is problematic, and its intensity varies from chapter to chapter, or even from page to page. Joyce felt at liberty to deal with Homer as highhandedly as Virgil had done, keeping the basic typology but varying and omitting and adding as his own book required. In the first episodes he realized his ambition of rendering the thousand complexities in the mind, and for the first time in literature we have all the lapses and bursts of attention, hesitations, half-recollections, distractions, sudden accesses or flaggings of sexual interest, feelings of hunger or nausea, somnolence, sneezing, thoughts about money, responses to the clouds and sunlight, along with the complications of social behavior and work. Joyce's power is shown not only in the density of sensations, but in the poetry and humor that infuse the principal characters and in the spirited irony of the narrator. Yet to mention these characteristics is to be put in mind of others. There is an extraordinary counterpoint between the first three chapters dealing with Stephen Dedalus and the next three dealing with Bloom. Not only is there an implicit parallel in their responses at the same hours of the day, but in the inner nature of the incidents that are described. So at the start of the first chapter, Buck Mulligan, holding a shaving bowl as if it were a chalice, claims to be transubstantiating the lather in it into the body and blood of Christ. Bloom makes an unspoken derisive commentary on this miracle when, at the end of the fourth chapter, he has a bowel movement and so in effect transubstantiates food into feces. Stephen ponders the way that states and churches alike have engaged in persecution and sadistic war, while Bloom thinks about the masochism which attracts devotees to confess and ask for punishment. A recognition of sado-masochism seems to bind the characters together, though they have not yet met. Then Stephen, as he walks along the strand and sees the debris heaped up by the waves, thinks darkly of the process of life as one from birth to decay to death. In the parallel passage in Bloom's morning, he attends a funeral, and is put in mind of the process from death through decay to new birth. What we thought were two parallel lines prove to be a circle.

As the book proceeds, the circle is itself questioned and

sometimes mocked. And the reign of order gives way to the reign of chaos. The physical universe, so glancingly built up in all its multiplicity in the early episodes, begins to lose its plausibility. Space and time, once so distinct, are shaken almost out of recognition. The reader like the narrative is caught up in the agitations and images of the unconscious mind. Our daytime selves are almost overwhelmed by this night. Yet in all the disorder Joyce keeps as firm a hand as he had when all was order in the early chapters. At the end he gives us back our world, somewhat the worse for wear, based no longer upon primal certitude but upon affirmation in the face of doubt, as the universe hangs upon the void. And while he prided himself on his novel's physicality, and ended with a supposedly fleshly monologue, what we recognize in reading Molly Bloom's soliloquy is that she is no fleshlier than Hamlet, and that for her too the mind affects everything. In it she acknowledges grudgingly that her husband, who recognizes her wit and musical talent and inner nature, is a better man than her lover Blazes Boylan. She pays Bloom the ultimate compliment, one a man rarely hears from a woman, "I saw he understood or felt what a woman is." Penelope recognizes Ulysses not by his scar but by his imagination. Although Joyce said jocularly of Molly that she is the flesh that always affirms, she is not to be identified with unconsciousness, or Mother Nature, or fertility. Her amorous career has been limited. She has copulated a little, she has ruminated a great deal. Bodies do not exist without minds. Molly may not be capable of impersonal thought, as Bloom is, but she has a good sharp practical intelligence. She is in fact cerebral too—a great and unexpected tribute from a writer who in life said many unpleasant things about women.

Joyce thought of his books as way stations on a psychic journey. His last book, *Finnegans Wake,* was an even more "extravagant excursion into forbidden territory," since it invaded the region of language itself, a region which other novelists had left

James Joyce, about 1933

inviolate. Dante obliged Italian literature to use the vernacular instead of Latin. Joyce's invention of *Finnegans-Wake*-ese was not intended to change literature so fundamentally, though it has had its imitators. Rather he wished to find an adequate medium to describe the world of night, the world of dream, the world of the unconscious, the world of madness. In such an atmosphere neither shapes nor events nor words could be intact. As he wrote in a letter, "One great part of every human existence is passed in a state which cannot be rendered sensible by the use of wideawake language, cutanddry grammar and goahead plot." Every person experiences this other state, but Joyce also envisaged a "universal history" in which he would represent the night world of humanity. This night world had always been associated with dark fantasies, but no one had described its work. The principal work of the night shift of humanity—its involuntary, accidental, half-conscious labor—is the perpetual de-creation and re-creation of language. The tongue slips, no one knows why. We go to sleep speaking Latin and wake up speaking French. Words break up, combine with words mysteriously imported from other languages, play tricks upon their own components. In the twinkling of a closed eye a red rose becomes a red nose, a phoenix becomes a finish, a funeral becomes a funforall. Joyce insisted that he was working strictly in accordance with the laws of phonetics, the only difference being that he accomplished in one fictional night what might take hundreds of years to occur through gradual linguistic change. He commented to a friend, Jacques Mercanton, "I reconstruct the life of the night the way the Demiurge goes about his creation, on the basis of a mental scenario that never varies. The only difference is that I obey laws I have not chosen. And he?" (He did not continue.) When people complained that the puns he was obliged by his scenario to use were trivial he made the famous retort, "Yes, some of my means are trivial, and some are quadrivial." When they said his puns were childish, he accepted the supposed blame with alacrity. He prided himself on not having grown up. His voice, he said, had never changed in adolescence. "It's because I've not developed. If I had matured, I wouldn't be so committed to the *folie* of writing *Work in Progress*." Keeping the child in the man gave him access to the universe which adults repressed.

In these ways Joyce radicalized literature, so that it would never recover. He reconstituted narrative, both external and internal; he changed our conception of daytime consciousness and of nighttime unconsciousness. He made us reconsider language as the product and prompter of unconscious imaginings. These did not come to him as experiments or as innovations; he did not regard himself as an experimenter. Rather they were solutions to the literary and intellectual problems he set himself.

Yet though his determination to change the way we think about ourselves and others as well as the way we read required the most elaborate methods, Joyce always insisted that his means were one thing, his meaning another. Complication was not in itself a good. "Can you not see the simplicity which is at the back of all my disguises?" he asked his wife before they eloped together. He objected to slavishness and ignobility; he thought they were fostered by conventional notions of heroism, which turned men and women into effigies. He wished them to know themselves as they really were, not as they were taught by church and state to consider themselves to be. He gave dignity to the common life that we all share. As he wrote to his brother, "Anyway my opinion is that if I put down a bucket into my own soul's well, sexual department, I draw up Griffith's and Ibsen's and Skeffington's and Bernard Vaughan's and St. Aloysius' and Shelley's and Renan's water along with my own. And I am going to do that in my novel (inter alia) and plank the bucket down before the shades and substances above mentioned to see how they like it: and if they don't like it I can't help them." Yet he was not impervious to those other qualities people also held in common, moments of exaltation and lyricism as important as they were infrequent.

He made no personal claims. "A man of small virtue, inclined to extravagance and alcoholism" was how he described himself to the psychologist Jung. He disclaimed genius, disclaimed imagination, only asserted that when he was writing his mind was as nearly normal as possible (November 10, 1907). He wished to give his contemporaries, especially his Irish ones, a good look at themselves in his polished looking glass—as he said—but not to destroy them. They must know themselves in order to become freer and more alive. Shear away adhesion to conventions and shibboleths, and what have we left? More, I think, than Lear's forked animal. We have the language-making and -using capacity, we have affections and disaffections, we have also humor, through which we tumble to our likeness to others. That likeness is seen in sad as well as joyful moments. The function of literature, as Joyce and his hero Stephen Dedalus both define it with unaccustomed fervor, is the eternal affirmation of the spirit of man, suffering and rollicking. We can shed what he called "laughtears" as his writings confront us with this spectacle.

Samuel Beckett

Samuel Beckett:
Nayman of Noland

SAMUEL BECKETT is *sui generis,* a writer with his own stamp, assured and stylized. This said, he can still usefully be ranged against his Irish predecessors. Because of what he has written, they take on a different look. Because of their work, he may seem not quite so rootless as he first appears. Although Beckett has not called attention to his Irish nationality as Yeats and Joyce did, his books are apt to mention with fondness unexpected Irish details. For example, in his first publication, the poem "Whoroscope," he draws in two brothers named Boot from seventeenth-century Dublin so as to compliment them for having refuted Aristotle. His character Molloy suddenly remarks, "Da, in my part of the world, means father," and the name Molloy reminds us of Beckett's conspicuous fondness for the commonest Irish names, especially if they begin with *M*—Murphy, Molloy, Moran. In his *Fizzles* the Irish word *deasil* (which means *clockwise*) suddenly appears, and we recall that it is also used conspicuously as the first word in the Oxen of the Sun episode in *Ulysses.* Beckett's translations of his works into English tend to give them an Irish inflection. When someone asked him if he were an Englishman, he replied, *"Au contraire."* These inclinations to acknowledge his Irish antecedents were qualified by his decision in early youth to live outside of Ireland. At the age of twenty-two Beckett went from Dublin to Paris; twenty-six years before, at the age of twenty, Joyce made the same journey. Equally pivotal were the displacements of Yeats at twenty-two from Dublin to London, and of Wilde, at twenty, from Dublin to Oxford. The geographical change symbolized for all four of them an attempt to proceed from the known to the unknown, to remake themselves in unfamiliar air.

When Beckett arrived in Paris in 1928, he might well have supposed that the principal outposts of literature had already been stormed, some of them by his own countrymen. Disapprove as he did of Yeats when he postured—for Beckett hates posturing—he could not help but find Yeats's late verse and prose incongruous with that poet's frequent references to his decrepitude. Joyce, whom Beckett soon met in Paris, had reconstructed prose narrative and, not content with radical modifications of English, was evolving "heavenly vocables" in a language never before uttered by man. Other eminences, of other nationalities, were of course about, and activity in related arts was intense. Beckett was not intimidated. Initially he pursued the academic career which he had earlier marked out for himself. He wrote about Proust and Joyce, in partisan and cryptic terms; he worked, or disdained to work, at a thesis in French literature; and after two years as *lecteur* at the Ecole Normale he went back to teach at Trinity College, Dublin.

His friends suspected that he was a genius, yet no one knew as yet how his abilities would be deployed. His teaching post at Trinity he quit abruptly because he discovered, and would later remark, that he could not teach others what he did not himself understand, a handicap that most of us endure without bridling. He returned to the continent, he traveled, he idled, he absorbed languages while he idled, he allowed himself amorous entanglements, and because there was nothing else for it and he was, as he liked to say later, "in the last ditch," he began to write. Whether he did it to express nuances or to exorcise demons he could perhaps not have specified. But write he did. First he was a poet who wrote short stories, then a novelist who wrote plays. Compositions of all kinds—often hard to label in traditional terms of genre—sprang from his sense that the old relations of authors to their subjects, to their characters, to their language, to their readers, and even to their own selves were discredited. Each foray into a more stark and final apprehension necessitated another; he was impatient with his own modes of pursuit, which became increasingly outlandish as he strove to come closer to the total expression of his experience. Not that he thought of himself as pursuing, for the idea of pursuer and quarry belonged to the past of literature. Rather he happened upon certain consequences of his own being. The urge to write seized him convulsively rather than on some Trollopian schedule.

The temporal stirrings of Beckett's molar genius are familiar. He published his first novel, *Murphy*, in 1938. That it was an early work seems to be demonstrated by its having a plot, though the plot was as he said deliberately hard to follow in its later stages. The character of Murphy in some ways extrapolated Beckett's own. Murphy is in search of plenitude, or is it emptiness? Perhaps they are the same. Beckett's work was to rest, or to be restless, amid such paradoxes. A corollary is that poverty and possessions are the same thing, possessions being only meaningless arrests in time, and time itself an illusion. Murphy, even more than Belacqua in the earlier short stories of *More Pricks than Kicks*, is someone to whom such paradoxes offer a way of life, or of non-life. Action is suspiciously like inaction, being like non-being. At the novel's start Murphy, self-bound by seven scarves in a rocking chair and attempting to rock himself (as Baudelaire says) "anywhere out of this world," feels the rocking chair overturn. Physical dislodgement and spiritual aspiration intermix, as if the world might overcome and be overcome at the same moment.

Beckett has encouraged us to think of his life not as a well-filled chronicle but as a patch of dark color. Authors, he has said, are never interesting. The poem "Whoroscope" about Descartes offers a monologue, fragmented and opaque. He was dissatisfied with the anodynes—love, ambition, diligence—with which we moderate incomprehension and futility. He agreed with Dr. Johnson, about whom he started to write a play, that the predominant element in life is misery, "I suffer, therefore I may be," was his improvement upon Descartes, as if misery marked but did not confirm existence, and as if thinking were out of the question. He suffered not only for himself but for others. His character Belacqua feels pity for the lobster thrown into the boiling pot, but Beckett's companionable sympathy extends beyond crustaceans. Forty-odd years after the event, he can still mourn the killing of

Jewish friends by the Nazis as if it had happened yesterday. That Estragon in *Waiting for Godot* was originally called Levy suggests some of the emotional origins of that play—though indeed the play's final form still embodies them. His dedication of the recent play *Catastrophe* to the dissident Czech dramatist Vaclav Havel indicates that Beckett sees horror as maintaining itself in post-Nazi events.

Both *Murphy* and a novel he wrote in English during the war, *Watt,* brought the characters to insane asylums, as if only there did human gestures approximate to their environment. Beckett was searching out a form for what he called "the mess." The mess could be framed if not alleviated. Shortly after the war in Europe had ended, he experienced what he would later with some embarrassment and yet some stubbornness identify as "a revelation." It occurred when he was visiting his mother in Ireland in the summer of 1945. In her house, "New Place," across the road from "Cooldrinagh" where he had grown up, he suddenly saw what his future writing must be. Unlike most revelations, this one offered no new heaven or new earth. If anything, something like a present hell. We know what the revelation was in part because Beckett himself satirized it in *Krapp's Last Tape.* This play manipulates the double perspective of Krapp young, taping his achievements, and Krapp old, exasperated with his earlier pretensions and eager to listen only to a memory of relinquished love. Krapp turns to box 3, spool 5, and hears his own claim made long before to have had such a momentous experience as Beckett did:

> Spiritually a year of profound gloom and indigence until that memorable night in March, at the end of the jetty, in the howling wind, never to be forgotten, when suddenly I saw the whole thing. The vision at last. This I fancy is what I have chiefly to record this evening, against the day when my work will be done and perhaps no place left in my memory, warm or cold, for the miracle...[hesitates] ...for the fire that set it alight. What I suddenly saw then was that, that the belief I had been going on all my life, namely...

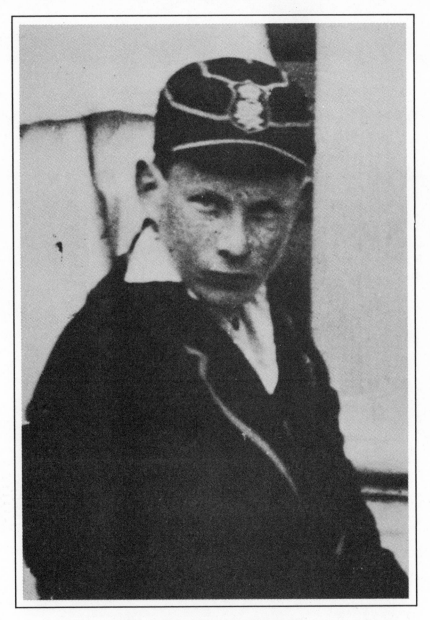

Beckett at Portora Royal School, Enniskillen

"Cooldrinagh," the house at Foxrock in the Dublin suburbs, where Beckett grew up

At this point he impatiently switches ahead on the tape, but not far enough, for we pick up the words, "that the dark I have always struggled to keep under is in reality my most..." before he switches again. The tape must have gone on to say, "that the dark I have always struggled to keep under is in reality my most" effective ally (or most valued confederate). What Krapp really wants to listen to is not his revelation, which no longer interests him, but his experience of a moment of love in a boat. He gets to this and listens to it with intentness. The tape relentlessly winds on past it:

Here I end this reel. Box three, spool five. Perhaps my best years are gone. When there was a chance of happiness. But I wouldn't want them back. Not with the fire in me now. No, I wouldn't want them back.

Constipated Krapp—banana-eating, spool-playing Krapp— would of course give anything to have them back. The fire of creation, if ever there was one, has long since gone out. Beckett memorializes here, with self-lacerating irony, a moment when he too must have made a crucial choice.

The label he gave to his new motive in art was poverty or impoverishment. His characters would be deprived not only of money but of youth, of health, of fortitude. I do not think that the aged, the infirm, the enervated attracted him for their own sake so much as because through them he could approach the underside of experience, go beneath pose and posture. His books would also neglect the available saving graces of literature. Since Balzac, novelists had prided themselves on amassing particulars. Beckett does not renounce them, though he speaks of doing so, but the particulars he includes, such as sucking stones, are of such paltriness that we scarcely notice them. Yet beds, chairs, pets, bikes, farts, and food appear, diverse and isolated. The furniture may not be Louis Quinze, but it is there. Only in one way did he allow himself an unexpected sumptuousness, and that was in language. He uses hard words that have to be looked up and then turn out to be marvelously apposite; he will not allow clichés or stock phrases to pass as dead matter; his sentences may describe faltering, but they themselves stand up under inspection; as if to counter the dying fall of his characters, his language undergoes a tremendous revivification. Beyond that, he deals in unheroics. His dislike of pretenses and pretensions makes him shy away from swelling chords towards diminuendoes. No makers and shapers, no deeds or events; nothing but residues, detritus, débris, the pratfall triumphant. It was one way of coming close to the nucleus of being, where the least false is the most true, where—as for Genet—the poorest is the richest, or as for Chaplin, the most painful is the funniest. In *More Pricks than Kicks* Belacqua asks himself, "Was it to be laughter or tears?...It came to the same thing in the end." Or as Oscar Wilde said, "There is a grotesque horror about its [life's] comedies, and its tragedies seem to culminate in farce." The two elements heighten each other.

Uncommon as Beckett's revelation was, his Irish predecessors appear to have experienced comparable moments of visionary decisiveness. The exact date of each is hard to discover and scarcely matters. With Joyce it was earlier than with Beckett; it came when he discovered the "epiphany," a term as portentous as revelation. An epiphany was the sudden and unostentatious exposure and disclosure of what some passing moment meant. The artist did not concoct it or interpret it, he simply apprehended its shape. While such moments might include dreams or lyrical intimations, the less expected ones were ugly and vulgar—pawn tickets or defecation for instance. The epiphany exalted the commonplace, and led naturally to the internal monologue, in which the essence of a situation was expressed seemingly without prior ordering, the epiphany personalized. With the epiphany Joyce discovered the world of the unmentionable and the not worth mentioning. Beckett's revelation led him to extend the unmentionable to the world of flagging energies.

For Wilde and Yeats too there appears to have been such a moment of revelation. When Wilde was first at Oxford, he berated himself for his opposite tendencies towards the heights of aspiration and the depths of sensation. The issue was crystallized for him by his desire to become a Catholic and his wish to be a pagan. He blamed himself for yielding to such a contrariety of impulse. But then there came a time when he saw that he might choose both rather than one or the other, and by living a kind of double life could avoid closing off an area of his own individuality. He acquired the courage that Baudelaire prayed for, to contemplate his own nature without disgust. His contemporaries might have their world of decision-making and conformity, but in having it they had to deny another world of secret impulse and furtive doubt. At some point Wilde came to see that this undisclosed aspect of experience might include sexual deviation, and deviation became a symbol of his acceptance of himself for what he was. It was as if every statement, like every proclivity, contained its own contradiction. To acknowledge this was to assure himself of a new source of insight; to present it to others the best medium was paradoxical wit. The paradox was an insistent reminder of what lay behind the accepted or conventional. Like Beckett, Wilde forces us to see beneath the surface of casual converse while keeping its structures intact. By the time he was thirty-two, his views on homosexuality, epigrams, and artistic insight had coalesced into a working method from which emerged his best writing. Only when he committed himself to a double life, and a double view, did he devise characters who disclosed or discovered that they were not what they seemed, so that Lady Windermere could act in complete disregard of her fixed principles, Algernon and Jack could imagine alternate lives for themselves, and Dorian Gray could find doubleness an affliction. Wilde did not invent a new language, as Joyce eventually felt compelled to do, but he evolved an English that challenged solemnities by its tautness and surprise.

Precisely when Yeats came to a realization of his nature and direction is harder to determine, but his friend George Russell said that in 1884, when nineteen, Yeats had been greatly excited by Russell's drawing of a man on a mountain, startled at his own image in the mist. It anticipated his own lifetime exploration of self and antiself, or pose and mask. By extension it included all the encroachments of fairies, spirits, demons, and images upon things of this world. Gautier said that he was one for whom the visible world existed; Yeats knew himself to be one for whom the invisible world existed. Just what the status of that invisible world was he could never state with definiteness. It was not like Wilde's double life, for in Yeats's case there were not two sexual directions but two scales for weighing reality. To encompass his gradually increasing sense of bifurcation he needed a new vocabulary and syntax, and these he molded in his late thirties.

The new language that Beckett found was an old one, French. The first pages that he composed after the Dun Laoghaire revelation, before he left Ireland once more, were in French, as he began his trilogy. The linguistic decision entailed quite different modes of expression to go with the new shapes of literature that he was evolving. His boldness was almost without precedent. It freed him from literary forefathers. It was a decision only less radical than Joyce's in inventing his extravagant *Finnegans Wake*-ese. Impoverishing himself, Beckett had to forswear all those associations which a native speaker writing in his own language happily makes use of. He has said that writing French freed him from the necessity of style, although in fact he evolved a new style in his adopted language.

The three novels of the trilogy, *Molloy, Malone Dies,* and *The Unnamable,* show their protagonists withering away along with the world they inhabit. Even their names become confused and finally disappear. Whether they have ever lived is also dubious. Beckett takes doubt to the point that David Hume reached but preferred to withdraw from. "My waking was a kind of sleeping," says Molloy with bitter wit. "I have lived in a kind of coma," is Malone's admission. "Let us go on," says the Unnamable, "as if I were the only one in the world, whereas I am the only one absent from it." While most artists concentrate on peopling the void, Beckett's creative act is unpeopling it again. "I can't go on, I'll go on," says the Unnamable, and some have seen this as a ray of hope in the Cimmerian darkness. To repudiate such a suggestion, forlorn as it is, Beckett ends his latest work with the terminal words, "Nohow on."

100

Beckett in the 1930s

The last page of the manuscript of En Attendant Godot

Beckett's characters generally hobble about, as far from the world of trains and trams as they can get. They are usually old, and mostly ill. Disease and old age have not been favorite literary subjects. Swift portrayed the superannuated in his Struldbrugs, who however do not speak; Beckett's Struldbrugs do little else. The speaker in his recent work, *Ill Seen Ill Said,* hopes that at the moment of expiring she will at last "know happiness." Perhaps no one has written so well as Beckett about how it feels to be so ill. He has given a voice to the decrepit and maimed and inarticulate, men and women at the end of their tether, past pose or pretense, past claim of meaningful existence. He seems to say that only there and then, as metabolism lowers, amid God's paucity, not his plenty, can the core of the human condition be approached. These lean and slippered pantaloons, crutched, paralyzed, defeated, are past the illusions which animal vigor proffers. Neither subjective nor objective worlds can maintain themselves in the face of decrepitude. "I say, I. Unbelieving," says the Unnamable and "It, say it, not knowing what." In *Worstward Ho* the figures of an old man and a child appear tentatively. "Any other would do as ill," the text confides. In *Company,* the first member of this most recent triad of Beckett's writings, the companions are imagined into a precarious existence from which they soon fade and leave their imaginer as he was at the start, alone. The imagination finds images to conceive of a world without them.

While he was carrying his trilogy of novels through to what we can only call (if we are true Beckettians) incompletion, in the 1940s, Beckett also composed two plays. The first has never been published, though we can get a good idea of it from Ruby Cohn's description. It was entitled *Eleuthéria*—Greek for *liberty.* Beckett's use of such a term is of necessity ironical, as far as possible from Byron fighting for Greek freedom at Missolonghi. It is centered on a young man who might be characterized as an anti-artist, and the play offers his portrait. This hero does not aspire through silence, exile, and cunning to forge a conscience for his race. The freedom he wishes for is simply to be rid of the world and his own selfhood. This freedom he will never achieve. The faint sound of his chains rubbing together will be as he says the closest to freedom he can get. Beckett must have had in mind to write a reverse *Bildungspiel,* not a shaping but a losing of shape, diseducation rather than education. (Shelley's Demogorgon tells us that "the deep truth is imageless.") Beckett put the play aside, perhaps because it was too much a counterstatement to Joyce's *A Portrait of the Artist.* After a time he set out to write, again in French, *Waiting for Godot.* In this play there could be no suspicion of Joyce's influence even being repudiated. Where *Eleutheria* dealt with the cancellation of relations among people, *Godot* deals with their futile continuance. In Beckett's prose fiction, doubles or near-doubles are likely to turn up; in his plays he usually summons up a more variegated world of down-and-outers, clowns, nihilists. The bleak but comic world they inhabit has the same foul weather as the novels. In the give-and-take of dialogue the characters complain of the same enigmatic confusion of reality and unreality, of point and pointlessness.

With *Waiting for Godot* Beckett framed his landscape and his mood. They were as memorable as Kafka's, yet different in that Kafka's people struggle purposefully, while Beckett's endure purposelessly. Waiting for them is like willing for others; they linger, uncertain why. They seem to be on the verge of discovering why they should not be there. Yet as with Kafka and with Henri Michaux—writers with whom Beckett has affinities—a certain aesthetic sense remains when the five physical senses more or less give way. "Let's abuse each other" and "Let's contradict each other" are games that Estragon and Vladimir are still willing to play. They take a wry satisfaction in their proficiency at them. In a later play, *Endgame,* Hamm tells himself, "You cried for night; it falls, now cry in darkness," and then compliments himself, "Nicely put, that." He has complimented himself on his phrasing earlier in the play, too. The language is alerted to itself as language. In the trilogy of novels, also, Malone congratulates himself on having phrased a problem, "nicely posed, I think, nicely indeed." There is a pleasure in expressing how hopeless is the future, as well as the present. Faced with the unbearable, men and women preposterously find a phrase for it. This aesthetic sense is related to Beckett's comic mode, in which even his most distressful works at times participate. Misery is particularized with such attentiveness, with

Beckett rehearsing

so many complex ramifications, as to become funny. Molloy has his sucking stones, Vladimir and Estragon have their boots.

Beckett is such an odd fish that his position vis à vis his predecessors is not easy to define. "The artist who stakes his being is from nowhere, has no kith," says Beckett in his essay on the painter Jack B. Yeats. The Unnamable aspires "to start again from nowhere, from no one, and from nothing." Reading Wilde, Yeats, and Joyce does not make the coming of Beckett predictable. Yet once he fills the scene we cannot help but consider or reconsider the writers who preceded him. And when we do, a strange thing happens. However unlike him they were, at least some of their interests appear to be proleptic of his. Qualities in his predecessors which had previously been less conspicuous he pushes to the fore.

Among the three Wilde, though he shared Beckett's middle-class, Protestant upbringing as well as his school and university, is the furthest afield. That insouciant boulevardier with his button-holed flower might appear to have nothing in common with Beckett's anxious alleycrawlers. Yet elegance and squalor call to each other as opposites. Flouting the work ethic and doing nothing are behavior patterns they have in common. It's true that Wilde's characters do nothing because they enjoy it, Beckett's because nothing is worth doing. Perhaps the distinction is not a small one. Life for Wilde is justified if during it art can be created, while in Beckett the creative impulse, though acknowledged, is impugned.

The mixture of erotic feeling and artistic ambition in *Krapp's Last Tape* may not be quite so distinct from Wilde as might be supposed. For Wilde also wrote an account of such a mixture and called it *De Profundis*. It could be described as Wilde's last tape. For in it as C.3.3 (his prison name) he remembers how as Oscar Wilde he kinged it, swaggering and successful, and as Wilde he looks at C.3.3, reduced and humbled. There is in it a good deal of self-examination, some pride in accomplishments, much remorse; much talk of earnest going forward. At the end Wilde seems to put these matters out of his mind as he turns to erotic thoughts of meeting Alfred Douglas again, just as Krapp furiously plays the tape ahead to his scene of love in a boat. The fire in Krapp has gone out, except for that, and in Wilde too the nub of his recollections is now, "The secret of life is suffering." He offers his newly apprehended summation of life as "Failure, disgrace, poverty, sorrow, despair, suffering, tears..." Beckett could not have known that when Wilde was composing *De Profundis* in Reading Gaol the warder each day removed the pages he had completed, but in *Molloy* we learn that Molloy's pages are removed each week in the same way.

That the secret of life is suffering was not something disclosed to Wilde only in prison. From his fairy tale, "The Happy Prince," through *Dorian Gray* and the character of Herod in *Salome*, there is a theme of anguished physical or spiritual decay. Herod, like Hamm in *Endgame*, retains an aesthetic sense as the world collapses around him. (In *Salome* Iokanaan rises from his cistern as Clov and Nell from their trash barrels in *Endgame*, a point I mention not to impute an influence but to suggest that both Wilde and Beckett could see drama in strange repositories.) One of Wilde's prose poems might serve as an epigraph to Beckett's work. It is the story of a sculptor who was commissioned to sculpt a work entitled, "The Sorrow That Endureth for Ever." Unfortunately he could find no bronze with which to make it, not anywhere in the land. At last he bethought himself of a work he had executed earlier entitled, "The Joy That Abideth Only for an Instant." So he melted the bronze of "The Joy That Abideth Only for an Instant" to fashion out of it "The Sorrow That Endureth for Ever." Beneath much posturing in Wilde there is much pain.

The closest connection between Wilde and Beckett may well be their propensity to use their art as recreation as well as vocation. Amid solemnities their characters are Irish enough to dawdle for a chat, or a cigarette, or something to eat. There is always time to split hairs. The slanging matches of Vladimir and Estragon find a parallel in the stichomythia, and the self-conscious taking part in a game, of Cicely and Gwendolyn in *The Importance of Being Earnest*, or of Lord Illingworth and Lady Allenby in *A Woman of No Importance*. Algernon's cucumber sandwiches, or Gilbert's ortolans in "The Critic as Artist," have counterparts in Beckett's coarser delicacies—Krapp's bananas, Vladimir's carrots. Both writers refresh the banal by bursting through the surface of statements, by taking an accepted idiom like "as well" and turning it into "as ill." "Having lost one leg," says the Unnamable, "what indeed more likely than that I should mislay the other?" and Lady Bracknell tells Jack, "To lose one parent may be regarded as a misfortune. To lose both looks like carelessness." Both writers incessantly play with language, so that *Westward Ho* can become *Worstward Ho* just as the adjective *earnest* gives a wry twist to the proper name *Ernest*. Puns of language connect with puns of identity. Dorian and his picture, the putative portrait of Willie Hughes and the Shakespearean sonnet about a man of all hues, in "The Picture of Mr. W. H.," provide visual as well as verbal puns. The manufacture of alternate selves is a leading enterprise for both writers. Beckett speaks of "existence by proxy." His proxies are sometimes humorous, like Bim and Bom in *Murphy*, but they can be sinister, as in *How It Is*, where the protagonist malevolently invents and tortures Bim, and in *The Unnamable* where Worm and Mahood offer their shadowy counterfeits of the principal character.

A more profound resemblance is the quality possessed by both men of what might be called self-cancellation. They cannot think of one possibility without evoking its opposite and recognizing its equal claim. In one of his sonnets Wilde adapted a phrase of Pater ("Neither for Jehovah nor for his enemies,") to describe himself, "Neither for God nor for his enemies," and Beckett makes use of the same line in *Fizzles* when he writes, "Grey cloudless sky verge upon verge grey timeless air of those nor for God nor his enemies." Wilde concludes his essay "The Truth of Masks" by allowing that he does not believe all that he has said. "A truth in art is that whose contradictory is also true," he declares, and in fact the tenor of that essay, which is a plea for archeological accuracy in theater staging, is itself in sharp contradiction to a remark he made in another mood, "Where archeology begins, art ceases." Beckett, as skeptical of fiction as he is of fact, has Molloy end his long monologue, "Then I went back into the house and wrote, It is midnight. The rain is beating on the windows. It was not midnight. It was not raining." Affirmation and denial go hand in hand. In *The Picture of Dorian Gray* Sibyl Vane gives up the pretense of art so as to live entirely artlessly in this world, only to commit suicide, and Dorian tries to give up the conditions of existence and to live in the deathless (and therefore lifeless) world of art, only to commit suicide too. When Wilde repudiates nature, experience, and the ordinary self in favor of the perfection of art, there is an underlying intimation that artifice hangs on the edge of non-being. Deny reality to the one, it is hard to claim it for the other. When he asserts that masks are more real than faces, the solidity of both is put in question. "All those Murphys, Molloys and Malones do not fool me," says the Unnamable. The suspicion latent in nineteenth-century aestheticism is that its constructions may be only Potemkin villages, fiction redoubling fiction to cover an essential barrenness, which Wilde like Beckett identifies with misery. "There is something vulgar about all success. The greatest men fail, or seem to have failed," Wilde attests, and Beckett says, "To be an artist is to fail, as no other dare fail..." In this respect Wilde prepares unwittingly for Beckett's more flagrant belittlements of both life and art.

As a literary figure Wilde could arouse Beckett's sympathy only after his fall, when his suffering became overt rather than covert. Wilde belonged to the previous century. Beckett was more respectful of Yeats, who had performed the feat of transforming himself from a nineteenth-century writer into a twentieth-century one. Among Yeats's poems Beckett had distinct preferences. Those early ones in which Yeats summoned up what Beckett called "the attar of far off, most secret, and inviolate rose," he recommended correcting by "a good smell of dung." Yeats by this time agreed, for he introduced into his later verse "frogspawn," "old bottles, old rags, and a broken can," and "excrement." Yet among Yeats's early poems Beckett singled out unerringly the one that was most extraordinary, entitled, "He Wishes His Beloved Were Dead." It was a sentiment that Beckett would himself reframe in four of his best lines of verse:

> I would like my love to die
> and the rain to be falling on the graveyard
> and on me walking the streets
> mourning the first and last to love me

The last line read in the original French, "pleurant celle qui crut m'aimer," "mourning her who thought she loved me." It is a line that Yeats could not have written, not only because his love did not even think she loved him, but because he would not have ended a poem on so cavilling a thought. Doubt—which Beckett likes to call more esoterically *aporia*—was for Yeats something to get beyond if possible. Beckett sought bathos as Yeats sought climax.

Beckett and Yeats met only once, at Killiney south of Dublin, introduced by Thomas MacGreevy. At this single meeting in 1932 Yeats astonished Beckett by praising a passage from "Whoroscope." The passage Yeats quoted referred to Descartes' attitude towards the Virgin Mary:

> A wind of evil flung my despair of ease
> against the sharp spires of the one
> lady

The suggestion of helpless male love and female cruelty may have impressed Yeats as much as the startling imagery. In a subsequent reciprocation, Beckett quoted lines from Yeats's poem, "The Tower," in the text and in the title of his minidrama "...*but the clouds*..." In Yeats's poem this phrase is part of a kind of grand testament:

> Now shall I make my soul
> Compelling it to study
> In a learned school
> Till the wreck of body,
> Slow decay of blood,
> Testy delirium
> Or dull decrepitude,
> Or what worse evil come—
> The death of friends, or death
> Of every brilliant eye
> That made a catch in the breath—
> Seem but the clouds of the sky
> When the horizon fades,
> Or a bird's sleepy cry
> Among the deepening shades.

Beckett leaves out the soul-making and the determination, concentrating on the last lines. In his play a man is trying to evoke the

Beckett rehearsing Buster Keaton in the film O

remembered image of a woman, a Maud-Gonne-like figure, and from time to time she appears briefly on a screen, murmuring inaudibly the last lines of Yeats's poem. At last the man quotes.

> …but the clouds of the sky
> When the horizon fades,
> Or a bird's sleepy cry
> Among the deepening shades.

The effect is not one of realization, as in Yeats, but of unreality, or of reality too dim to be apprehended. In Beckett the clouds are triumphant, not the man, who is forever subject to decay of body, testy delirium, or dull decrepitude.

Most of Yeats's late work in verse and drama contained elements that were congenial to Beckett. There were aged bundles of memories, such as Crazy Jane and Mad Tom, images of senile lust, of love lost or gained long ago, of flat and fallen breasts, of old scarecrows resembling men, of people "ravening, raging, and uprooting" only to come "into the nothingness of reality." The sense of the world's transmutability into an imaginative paradise, which is strong in Yeats, was alien to Beckett; but in the obverse of that, which occurs in Yeats from time to time, he could find kinship. An ardent attender of plays at the Abbey Theater in Dublin, Beckett admired the late plays of Yeats. He liked especially the one about Swift in *The Words upon the Window-Pane*, in which the voice of Swift utters the devastating final line, "Perish the day on which I was born." He also liked Yeats's version of the Sophoclean plays about King Oedipus, an apt emblem for Beckett of the human situation in general—man blinded and dispossessed, like Hamm in *Endgame*. Another play that moved him was *At the Hawk's Well*, where an old man and a young one wait in vain, as do Estragon and Vladimir, for something that never happens to them. In *Happy Days* Winnie quotes from it, "I call to the eye of the mind." We can imagine Beckett sympathizing with the old man who, as Chorus in *The Death of Cuchulain*, concludes his prelude to the play with the words, "I spit! I spit! I spit!" Or with the scenery in Yeats's play *Purgatory* which rather like that of *Godot* consists of a blasted tree. The reduction of scenery, the elimination of flamboyant gesture, the concentration of words were to be characteristics of Beckett's theatre as they were of Yeats's. One need not overstate the bond between Yeats, with his fabulous occurrences in legendary places and anatomizing of the heroic, and Beckett, who has no truck with Irish legend and prefers the anatomy of the unheroic. Still, Yeats had a strain of skepticism too. His poems about Byzantium, artifice triumphant over nature, are balanced by poems about the void, in which all art is only what he magnificently calls "the cold snows of a dream." (Even in "Byzantium" the fire of art "cannot singe a sleeve.")

The relation of Beckett to Joyce is the hardest of the three to clarify. Hostile critics at first suggested that Beckett was Joyce's disciple, chiefly perhaps because his early books described characters wandering not very purposefully around cities. Such echoes as there are were mainly parodic. Beckett took over the Joycean monologue, but everyone has been doing that, and Joyce himself was following Dujardin. Certain kinds of humor, especially the painstaking enumeration of mechanical details, they both enjoyed, but so did Rabelais, and Chaplin.

Beckett probably knew Joyce as well as anyone during the last thirteen years of Joyce's life. They met often, they conversed frequently, though much of the time without words, directing silences across each other's torsos and into the unfeeling ether. Beckett has said that his short play *Ohio Impromptu* records their friendship. It refers to walks they took together along the Seine to the Ile des Cygnes. "With never a word exchanged they grew to be as one," it says. Beckett was almost the only young writer whose talent Joyce acknowledged, and when *Murphy* was published, Joyce paid it the compliment of a bad limerick, and more important, quoted to Beckett from memory the passage about the disposal of Murphy's ashes on the floor of a pub, the ashes mixing with the spit and sawdust and vomit in a way that Joyce, past master of the mixed mode and squalid imagery, could value.

For his part, Beckett recognized what he would later call Joyce's "heroic work, heroic being." None the less, he did not subscribe wholeheartedly to all Joyce's works. In particular he thought Stephen Dedalus's sense of mission too clamant, his own being based on abjuring claims. The play *Exiles* he found blood-

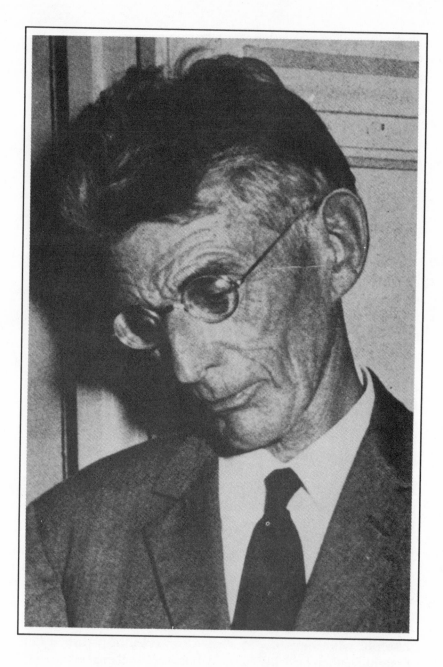

less. *Finnegans Wake,* the work on which Joyce was engaged during their friendship, provoked his admiration. Beckett was the first to try to translate it into another language, and he also wrote a defense of it at Joyce's request. Still, its point of view was not one with which he could altogether agree. That "yesterday shall be tomorrow" might be true, as *Finnegans Wake* implied, yet Beckett marveled at the way that Joyce seemed to make no distinction between the fall of Satan and the fall of a sparrow. Contemplating life from this perspective turned it all to sad and rollicking farce. Beckett could have agreed with Joyce's motto, "the seim anew," and in fact he begins *Murphy* with "nothing new" and ends *Worstward Ho* with "Nought anew." But the repetition did not arouse in him a feeling of tolerance or acceptance. So in an acrostic on Joyce he announced himself as a defector from the Joycean universe.

Joyce's attitude to language was another matter on which they differed. *Finnegans Wake* grew out of a wish that Joyce had expressed long before, for a language beyond national boundaries, one to which all known languages would be tributary. For such a language the polyglot tongue of *Finnegans Wake* offered at least a metaphor. Beckett could not celebrate the word in such terms. Since literature did not appear to him, as it did to Joyce and to Stephen Dedalus, to be the eternal affirmation of the spirit of man, language must suffer demotion also. The goal of speech in Beckett is not more speech. The mouth opens because it has to, and looks forward to being finally shut. "Words," he told Lawrence Harvey, "are a form of complacency." Beckett could find more sympathetic Bloom's contemplation of old age as a "grey sunken cunt"—the last word one of which Beckett particularly approves—in the Calypso episode of *Ulysses,* of "maggoty death" in the Hades episode, and of Joyce's version of the cruelty of the unconscious in the Circe episode. Very much to Beckett's taste was the death scene of Anna Livia Plurabelle as "sad and old" she finds herself rivering relentlessly into the salt sea.

I have tried to suggest how, in the age of Beckett, Wilde, Joyce, and Yeats take on some of his attributes. But if we regard him for a moment as their successor, even though like every great writer he comes from nowhere, our attitude towards him undergoes some change. In *Finnegans Wake* Joyce ironically described the type of the artist as "Nayman of Noland," existing on the vacuum of his own most intensely doubtful soul. Beckett might be said to embody this type, except for certain discrepancies. It is true that in *How It Is* he plays on Joyce's "work in progress" as "ruins in prospect." Yet as his predecessors' affirmations are challenged by his doubts, so his doubts may seem less scorching if he is read after them. In particular, his naysaying is accompanied by innumerable comic details.

To say no in thunder is one thing, to say no in vaudeville is another. Beckett has never been willing to say yes or no to the Nobel Prize committee's judgment that he had "transmuted the destitution of modern man into his exaltation." Certainly he did not set out with this goal in mind. But as Nietzsche says, "Only where there are tombs are there resurrections." It is somehow salutary to know the horrors in store for us. Joyce claimed to have given a voice to the third of human life that is spent in sleep. Beckett could claim to have given a voice to the third of every existence likely to be spent in decay. His studied reticence about his purpose is justified. To explain is to attenuate. As his writings have become shorter, he has seemed to imply that faithful images of life have to be squeezed out. Yet his musical cadences, his wrought and precise sentences, cannot help but stave off the void. Even here, as he says in *Ill Seen Ill Said*, "Imagination at wit's end spreads its sad wings." If he means to depress us merely, he may be said to outwit himself. Those sad wings are not only panache, they are also poise. Like salamanders we survive in his fire.

Acknowledgments

These four essays were delivered in different form as lectures at the Library of Congress under the auspices of the Gertrude Clarke Whittall Poetry and Literature Fund during a period of four years. That on Joyce was given on March 10, 1982; on Wilde, March 1, 1983; on Yeats, April 2, 1984; and on Beckett, April 16, 1985. They were published separately as pamphlets by the Library of Congress and as articles in the *New York Review of Books* before being revised and assembled in book form.

I wish to thank my hospitable hosts and my indulgent auditors.

"Oscar Wilde at Oxford": For various material I am indebted to Mary Hyde (Viscountess Eccles), Sir Rupert Hart-Davis, the William Andrews Clark Library of the University of California at Los Angeles, the University of Reading Library, and the Bodleian Library. Alon Kadish discovered the details of the Hardinge incident and kindly allowed me to mention them.

For the illustrations, I am grateful to the Prints and Photographs Division, Library of Congress, for pp. x, 5, and 15; the William Andrews Clark Library for pp. 6 and 9, and Mary Hyde for p. 19.

"W. B. Yeats's Second Puberty": I am grateful to Warwick Gould for giving me the text of Yeats's little poem about nothing, the original of which is now in his possession. It was dictated to Edith Shackleton Heald by Yeats and signed by him, and was part of a sale at Christie's in 1978. Michael Yeats remembered some of his father's late utterances. Mrs. Yeats, Norman Haire, and Frank O'Connor also contributed their recollections from the past. John F. Kelly helped with certain unpublished letters of Yeats.

For the illustrations, I am grateful to the Prints and Photographs Division, Library of Congress, for p. 26. All the rest I owe to the courtesy of the Special Collections Department, Robert W. Woodruff Library, Emory University.

"James Joyce In and Out of Art": James Atherton and Fritz Senn kindly put me in touch with the late Dr. Gertrude Kaempffer, to whom I owe the account of Joyce in Locarno. Professor Heinrich Straumann helped me with Joyce's association with Marthe Fleischmann. Frank Budgen shared his recollections of her with me. The Reverend Bruce Bradley, S.J., Rector of Belvedere College, showed me the Clongowes Punishment Book in which Joyce's name appeared three times.

For the illustrations, I am grateful to the Prints and Photographs Division, Library of Congress, for p. 74; and to the Henry W. and Albert A. Berg Collection, The New York Public Library (Astor, Lenox and Tilden Foundations) for p. 55. The rest are from my collection.

"Samuel Beckett: Nayman of Noland": Samuel Beckett told me of his meeting with Yeats and of his walks with Joyce.

For the illustrations, I am grateful to Samuel Beckett for p. 89; the Beckett Archive, Reading University for pp. 78, 83, 90, 93, 99, and 102; and Radio Telefis Eireann, with thanks to Séan Ó Mórdha, for pp. 84.

118

INDEX